I0018638

Changes and Bugs – Mining and Predicting Software Development Activities

Thomas Zimmermann

Changes and Bugs

Mining and Predicting Software Development Activities

Bibliografische Information der Deutschen Nationalbibliothek

Die Deutsche Nationalbibliothek verzeichnet diese Publikation in der Deutschen Nationalbibliografie; detaillierte bibliografische Daten sind im Internet über http://dnb.d-nb.de abrufbar.

Bibliographic information published by the Deutsche Nationalbibliothek

The Deutsche Nationalbibliothek lists this publication in the Deutsche Nationalbibliografie; detailed bibliographic data are available in the Internet at http://dnb.d-nb.de.

Author

Dr. Thomas Zimmermann (tz@acm.org), http://thomas-zimmermann.com.

Photo Credits

Cover page (front): "Meeting" ©iStockphoto.com/bodhihill (#5989636)
Cover page (back): "Bug on Grass" ©iStockphoto.com/bodhihill (#5989246)
Page iii: "Computer Bugs" ©iStockphoto.com/wolv (#1484508)
Page 5: "Chameleon Furcifer Pardalis – Ambilobe" ©iStockphoto.com/GlobalP (#6387850)
Page 59: "Ladybug and pebbles stack" ©iStockPhoto.com/arlindo71 (#7288107)
Page 109: "Ladybug Glasses" ©iStockphoto.com/bodhihill (#5989232)
Page 136: "About this Book in a Wordle" created with http://www.wordle.net/

Herstellung und Verlag: Books on Demand GmbH, Norderstedt

ISBN-13: 978-3-8391-0746-1

Contents

List of Figures

List of Tables

1

Introduction

The amount of data generated during software development is continuously increasing. According to the web-site CIA.vc every 26 seconds a change is reported for an open-source project. As of February 2008, the software development community SourceForge.net hosted 169,383 projects. Besides change, another constant in software development is to err. The bug databases of ECLIPSE and MOZILLA combined contain more 600,000 issue reports.

The availability of all this data recently led to a new research area called *mining software repositories (MSR)*. Both software practitioners and researchers alike use such data to understand and support software development and empirically validate novel ideas and techniques. A detailed survey on mining software repositories techniques was conducted by Kagdi et al. (2007). As they show, research on MSR is very interdisciplinary. Commonly used techniques come from applied statistics, information retrieval, artificial intelligence, social sciences, and software engineering. Their purpose is very diversified, ranging from empirical studies and change prediction to the development of tools in order to support programmers.

Two examples for MSR tools are *project memories* and *recommender systems*.

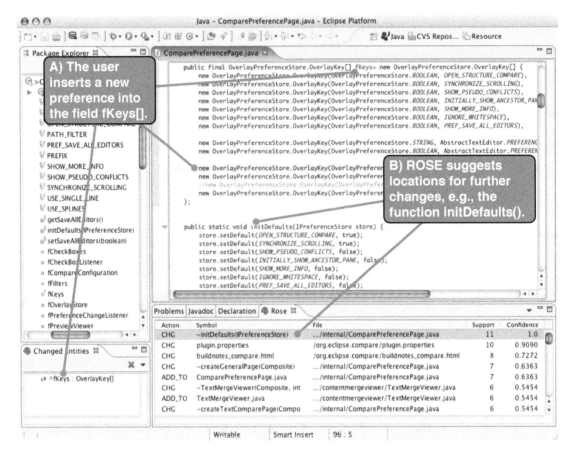

Figure 1.1: After a programmer has made some changes to the source (above), EROSE suggests locations (below) where, in the past further changes were made.

Project memories. The HIPIKAT tool recommends relevant software development artifacts, such as source code, documentation, bug reports, e-mails, changes, and articles based on the context in which a developer requests help. The project memory is built automatically and useful in particular for newcomers (Cubranic et al., 2005). The BRIDGE project at Microsoft is a comparable project within an industrial setting (Venolia, 2006a,b).

Recommender systems. Just like Amazon.com suggests related products after a purchase, the EROSE Eclipse plug-in guides programmers based on the change history of a project. Suppose a developer changed an array fKeys[]. EROSE then suggests to change the initDefaults() function—because in the past, both items always have been changed together. If the programmer misses to commit a related change, EROSE issues a warning (Zimmermann et al., 2005). While EROSE operates on change history as recorded in CVS, more recent tools relied on navigation data (DeLine et al., 2005; Singer et al., 2005).

This book makes two contributions to the body of MSR research. First, it mines fine-grained change for usage patterns and cross-cutting concerns (Part I). Second, it shows how to predict defects from dependency data, which help managers to allocate resources for quality assurance to the parts of a software that need it most (Part II).

1.1   Organization

This book is structured in two parts. The first part leverages version archives and mines for fine-grained changes, more precisely for *co-addition* of method calls, which is when two or more invocations to methods are introduced in the same CVS transaction.

Mining usage patterns.   A great deal of attention has always been given to addressing software bugs such as errors in operating system drivers or security bugs. However, there are many other lesser known errors specific to individual applications or APIs and these violations of application-specific coding rules are responsible for a multitude of errors.

We propose DYNAMINE, a tool that analyzes version archives to find highly correlated method calls (usage pattern). Potential patterns are passed to a dynamic analysis tool for validation. The combination of mining software repositories and dynamic analysis techniques proves effective for discovering new application-specific patterns and for finding violations in very large applications with many person-years of development. (Chapter 2)

Mining cross-cutting concerns.   Aspect mining identifies cross-cutting concerns in a program to help migrating it to an aspect-oriented design. Such concerns may not exist from the beginning, but emerge over time. By analyzing where developers add code to a program, our history-based aspect mining (HAM) identifies and ranks cross-cutting concerns. HAM scales up to industrial-sized projects: for example, we were able to identify a locking concern that cross-cuts 1,284 methods in ECLIPSE. Additionally, the precision of HAM is high; for ECLIPSE, it reaches 90% for the top-10 candidates. (Chapter 3)

The second part additionally takes information from bug databases into account and moves to an industrial setting.

In software development, resources for quality assurance are limited by time and by cost. In order to allocate resources effectively, managers need to rely on their experience backed by code complexity metrics (Chapter 4). But often dependencies exist between various pieces of code over which managers may have little knowledge. These dependencies can be construed as a low level graph of the entire system.

Predicting defects for binaries. We propose to use network analysis on dependency graphs to predict the number of defects for binaries. In our evaluation on Windows Server 2003, we found the recall for models built from network measures is by 10% points higher than for models built from complexity metrics. In addition, network measures could identify 60% of the binaries that the Windows developers considered as critical—twice as many as identified by complexity metrics. (Chapter 5)

Predicting defects for subsystems. We investigated the architecture and dependencies of Windows Server 2003 to show how to use the complexity of a subsystem's dependency graph to predict the number of failures at statistically significant levels. (Chapter 6)

Our techniques allows managers to identify central program units that are more likely to face defects. Such predictions can help to allocate software quality resources to the parts of a product that need it most, and as early as possible. The book concludes with a summary of its contributions and an outlook into future work (Chapter 7).

Part I

Mining Changes

2

Mining Usage Patterns

Many errors are specific to individual applications or platforms. Violations of these application-specific coding rules, referred to as *error patterns*, are responsible for a multitude of errors. Error patterns tend to be re-introduced into the code over and over by multiple developers working on a project and are a common source of software defects. While each pattern may be only responsible for a few bugs in a given project snapshot, when taken together over the project's lifetime, the detrimental effect of these error patterns can be quite serious and they can hardly be ignored in the long term if software quality is to be expected.

A great deal of attention has always been given to addressing application-specific software bugs such as errors in operating system drivers (Ball et al., 2004; Engler et al., 2000), security errors (Huang et al., 2004; Wagner et al., 2000), or errors in reliability-critical embedded software in domains like avionics (Blanchet et al., 2003; Brat and Venet, 2005). These represent critical errors in widely used software and tend to get fixed relatively quickly when found. A variety of static and dynamic analysis tools have been developed to address these high-profile bugs.

Finding the error patterns to look for with a particular static or dynamic analysis tool is often difficult, especially when it comes to legacy code, where error patterns either are documented as comments in the code or not documented at all (Engler et al., 2001). Moreover, while well-aware of certain types of behavior that causes the application to crash or well-publicized types of bugs such as buffer overruns, programmers often have difficulty formalizing or even expressing API invariants.

In this chapter we propose an automatic way to *extract likely error patterns* by mining software revision histories. Looking at incremental changes between revisions as opposed to complete snapshots of the source allows us to better focus our mining strategy and obtain more precise results. Our approach uses revision history information to infer likely error patterns. We then experimentally evaluate the patterns we extracted by checking for them dynamically.

We have performed experiments on ECLIPSE and JEDIT, two large, widely-used opensource Java applications. Both ECLIPSE and JEDIT have many man-years of software development behind them and, as a collaborative effort of hundreds of people across different locations, are good targets for revision history mining. By mining CVS, we have identified 56 high-probability patterns in the APIs of ECLIPSE and JEDIT, all of which were previously unknown to us. Out of these, 21 were dynamically confirmed as valid patterns and 263 pattern violations were found.

The rest of this chapter is organized as follows. Section 2.1 provides an informal description of DYNAMINE, our pattern mining and error detection tool. Section 2.2 describes our revision history mining approach. Section 2.3 describes our dynamic analysis approach. Section 2.4 summarizes our experimental results for (a) revision history mining and (b) dynamic checking of the patterns. Sections 2.5 and 2.6 present related work and summarize this chapter.

2.1   Overview of DYNAMINE

A great deal of research has been done in the area of checking and enforcing specific coding rules, the violation of which leads to well-known types of errors. However, these rules are not very easy to come by: much time and effort has been spent by researchers looking for worthwhile rules to check (Reimer et al., 2004) and some of the best efforts in error detection come from people intimately familiar with the application domain (Engler et al., 2000; Shankar et al., 2001). As a result, lesser known types of bugs and applications remain virtually unexplored in error detection research. A better approach is needed if we want to attack "unfamiliar" applications with error detection tools. This chapter proposes a set of techniques that automate the step of application-specific pattern discovery through revision history mining.

2.1.1 Motivation for Revision History Mining

Our approach to mining revision histories hinges on the following observation:

Observation 2.1 (Common Errors)
Given multiple software components that use the same API, there arc usually common errors *specific to that API.*

In fact, much of research done on bug detection so far can be thought of as focusing on specific classes of bugs pertaining to particular APIs: studies of operating-system bugs provide synthesized lists of API violations specific to operating system drivers resulting in rules such as "do not call the interrupt disabling function cli() twice in a row" (Engler et al., 2000).

In order to locate common errors, we mine for frequent usage patterns in revision histories, as justified by the following observation.

Observation 2.2 (Usage Patterns)
Method calls that are frequently added to the source code simultaneously often represent a pattern.

Looking at incremental changes between revisions as opposed to full snapshots of the sources allows us to better focus our mining strategy. However, it is important to notice that not every pattern *mined* by considering revision histories is an actual *usage pattern*. Figure 2.1 lists sample method calls that were added to revisions of files Foo.java, Bar.java, Baz.java, and Qux.java. All these files contain a usage pattern that says that methods {addListener, removeListener} must be precisely matched. However, mining these revisions yields additional patterns like {addListener, println} and {addListener, iterator} that are definitely *not* usage patterns.

Furthermore, we have to take into account the fact that in reality some patterns may be inserted incompletely, e.g., by mistake or to fix a previous error. In Figure 2.1 this occurs in file Qux.java, where addListener and removeListener were inserted independently in revisions 1.41 and 1.42. The observation that follows gives rise to an effective ranking strategy used in DYNAMINE.

File	Revision	Added method calls
Foo.java	1.12	o1.addListener o1.removeListener
Bar.java	1.47	o2.addListener o2.removeListener System.out.println
Baz.java	1.23	o3.addListener o3.removeListener list.iterator iter.hasNext iter.next
Qux.java	1.41	o4.addListener
	1.42	o4.removeListener

Figure 2.1: Method calls added across different revisions.

Observation 2.3 (One-line Fixes)
Small changes to the repository such as one-line additions often represent bug fixes.

This observation is supported in part by anecdotal evidence and also by recent research into the nature of software changes (Purushothaman and Perry, 2005) and is further discussed in Section 2.2.3.

To make the discussion in the rest of this section concrete, we present the categories of patterns discovered with our mining approach.

- **Matching method pairs** represent two methods for which the calls that must be precisely matched on all paths through the program.

- **State machines** are patterns that involve calling more than two methods on the same object and can be captured with a finite automaton.

- **More complex patterns** are all other patterns that fall outside the categories above and involve multiple related objects.

The categories of patterns above are listed in the order of frequency of high-likelihood pattern in our experiments. The rest of this section describes each of these error pattern categories in detail.

2.1.2 Motivation for Dynamic Analysis

Our technique for mining patterns from software repositories can be used independently with a variety of bug-finding tools. Our approach is to look for pattern violations at runtime, as opposed to using a static analysis technique. This is justified by several considerations outlined below.

- **Scalability.** Our original motivation was to be able to analyze ECLIPSE, which is one of the largest Java applications ever created. The code base of ECLIPSE is comprised of more than 2,900,000 lines of code and 31,500 classes. Most of the patterns we are interested in are spread across multiple methods and need an interprocedural approach to analyze. Given the substantial size of the application under analysis, precise whole-program flow-sensitive static analysis is expensive. Moreover, static call graph construction presents a challenge for applications that use dynamic class loading. In contrast, dynamic analysis does not require static call graph information.

- **Validating discovered patterns.** A benefit of using dynamic analysis is that we are able to "validate" the patterns we discover through CVS history mining as real usage patterns by observing how many times they occur at runtime. Patterns that are matched a large number of times with only a few violations represent likely patterns with a few errors. The advantage of validated patterns is that they increase the degree of assurance in the quality of mined results.

- **False positives.** Runtime analysis does not suffer from false positives because all pattern violations detected with our system actually *do* happen, which significantly simplifies the process of error reporting.

- **Automatic repair.** Finally, only dynamic analysis provides the opportunity to fix the problem on the fly without any user intervention. This is especially appropriate in the case of a matching method pair when the second method call is missing. While we have not implemented automatic "pattern repair" in DYNAMINE, we believe it to be a fruitful future research direction.

While we believe that dynamic analysis is more appropriate than static analysis for the problem at hand, a serious shortcoming of dynamic analysis is its lack of coverage. In fact, in our dynamic experiments, we have managed to find runtime use cases for some, but not all of our mined patterns. Another concern is that a workload selection may significantly influence how patterns are classified by DYNAMINE. In our experiments with ECLIPSE and JEDIT we were careful to exercise common functions of both applications that represent hot paths through the code and thus contain errors that may frequently manifest at runtime. However, we may have missed patterns that occur on exception paths that were not hit at runtime.

In addition to the inherent lack of coverage, another factor that reduced the number of patterns available for checking at runtime was that ECLIPSE contains much platform-specific code. This code is irrelevant unless the pattern is located in the portion of the code specific to the execution platform.

2.1.3   DYNAMINE System Overview

We conclude this section by summarizing how the various stages of DYNAMINE processing work when applied to a new application. All of the steps involved in mining and dynamic program testing are accessible to the user from within custom ECLIPSE views. A diagram representing the architecture of DYNAMINE is shown in Figure 2.2.

1. Pre-process revision history, compute methods calls that have been inserted, and store this information in a database.

2. Mine the revision database for likely usage patterns.

3. Present mining results to the user in an ECLIPSE plugin for assessment.

4. Generate instrumentation for patterns deemed relevant and selected by the user through DYNAMINE's ECLIPSE plugin.

5. Run the instrumented program and dynamic data is collected and post-processed by dynamic checkers.

6. Dynamic pattern violation statistics are collected and patterns are classified as validated usage patterns or error patterns. The results are presented to the user in ECLIPSE.

Steps 4–6 above can be performed in a loop: once dynamic information about patterns is obtained, the user may decide to augment the patterns and re-instrument the application.

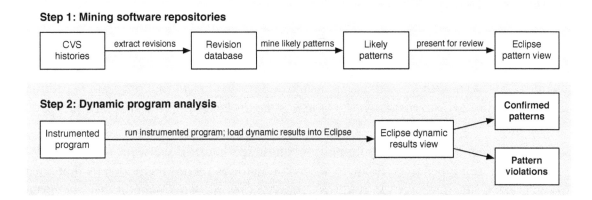

Figure 2.2: Architecture of DYNAMINE. The first row represents revision history mining. The second row represents dynamic analysis.

2.2   Mining Usage Patterns

In this section we describe our mining approach for finding usage patterns. We start by providing the terms we use in our discussion of mining. Next we lay out our general algorithmic approach that is based on the Apriori algorithm (Agrawal and Srikant, 1994; Mannila et al., 1994) that is commonly used in data mining for applications such as market basket analysis. The algorithm uses a set of *transactions* such as store item purchases as its input and produces as its output (a) frequent patterns ("items X, Y, and Z are purchased together") and (b) strong association rules ("a person who bought item X is likely to buy item Y").

However, the classical Apriori algorithm has a serious drawback. The algorithm runtime can be exponential in the number of items. Our "items" are names of individual methods in the program. For ECLIPSE, which contains 59,929 different methods, calls to which are inserted, scalability is a real concern. To improve the scalability of our approach and to reduce the amount of noise, we employ a number of filtering strategies described in Section 2.2.2 to reduce the number of viable patterns Apriori has to consider. Furthermore, Apriori does not rank the patterns it returns. Since even with filtering, the number of patterns returned is quite high, we apply several ranking strategies described in Section 2.2.3 to the patterns we mine. We start our discussion of the mining approach by defining some terminology used in our algorithm description.

Definition 2.1 (Usage Pattern)
A usage pattern $U = \langle M, S \rangle$ *is defined as a set of methods* M *and a specification* S *that defines how the methods should be invoked. A static usage pattern is present in the source if calls to all methods in* M *are located in the source and are invoked in a manner consistent with* S. *A dynamic usage pattern is present in a program execution if a sequence of calls to methods* M *is made in accordance with the specification* S.

The term "specification" is intentionally open-ended because we want to allow for a variety of pattern types to be defined. Revision histories record method calls that have been inserted together and we shall use this data to mine for method sets M. The fact that several methods are correlated does not define the nature of the correlation. Therefore, even though the exact pattern may be obvious given the method names involved, it is generally quite difficult to *automatically* determine the specification S by considering revision history data only and human input is required.

Definition 2.2 (Transaction)
For a given source file revision, a transaction is a set of methods, calls to which have been inserted.

Definition 2.3 (Support Count)
The support count of a usage pattern $U = \langle M, S \rangle$ *is the number of transactions that contains all methods in* M.

In the example in Figure 2.1 the support count for {addListener, removeListener} is 3. The changes to Qux.java do not contribute to the support count because the pattern is distributed across two revisions.

Definition 2.4 (Association Rule)
An association rule $A \Rightarrow B$ *for a pattern* $U = \langle M, S \rangle$ *consists of two non-empty sets* A *and* B *such that* $M = A \cup B$.

For a pattern $U = \langle M, S \rangle$ there exist $2^{|M|} - 2$ possible association rules. An association rule $A \Rightarrow B$ is interpreted as follows: whenever a programmer inserts calls to all methods in A, she also insert the calls of all methods in B. Obviously, such rules are not always true. They have a probabilistic meaning.

Definition 2.5 (Confidence)
The confidence of an association rule $A \Rightarrow B$ is defined as the the conditional probability $P(B|A)$ that a programmer inserts the calls in B, given the condition she has already inserted the calls in A.

The confidence indicates the *strength* of a rule. However, we are more interested in the patterns than in association rules. Thus, we rank patterns by the confidence values of their association rules (see Section 2.2.3).

2.2.1   Basic Mining Algorithm

A classical approach to compute frequent patterns and association rules is the Apriori algorithm (Agrawal and Srikant, 1994; Mannila et al., 1994). The algorithm takes a *minimum support count* and a *minimum confidence* as parameters. We call a pattern *frequent* if its support is above the minimum support count value. We call an association rule *strong* if its confidence is above the minimum confidence value. Apriori computes (a) the set P of all frequent patterns and (b) the set R of all strong association rules in two phases:

1. The algorithm iterates over the set of transactions and forms patterns from the method calls that occur in the same transaction. A pattern can only be frequent when its subsets are frequent and patterns are expanded in each iteration. Iteration continues until a fixed point is reached and the final set of frequent patterns P is produced.

2. The algorithm computes association rules from the patterns in P. From each pattern $p \in P$ and every method set $q \subseteq p$ such that $p, q \neq \emptyset$, the algorithm creates an association rule of the form $p - q \Rightarrow q$. All rules for a pattern have the same support count, but different confidence values. Strong association rules $p - q \Rightarrow q$ are added to the final set of rules R.[1]

In Sections 2.2.2 and 2.2.3 below we describe how we adapt the classic Apriori approach to improve its scalability and provide a ranking of the results.

---

[1]The rest of the book uses $-$ to denote set difference.

2.2.2   Pattern Filtering

The running time of Apriori is greatly influenced by the number of patterns is has to consider. While the algorithm uses thresholds to limit the number of patterns that it outputs in P, we employ some filtering strategies that are specific to the problem of revision history mining. Another problem is that these thresholds are not always adequate for keeping the amount of noise down. The filtering strategies described below greatly reduce the running time of the mining algorithm *and* significantly reduce the amount of noise it produces.

2.2.2.1   Considering a Subset of Method Calls Only

Our strategy to deal with the complexity of frequent pattern mining is to ignore method calls that either lead to no or only to obvious usage patterns such as {hasNext, next}.

- **Ignoring initial revisions.** We do not treat initial revisions of files as additions. Although they contain many usage patterns, taking initial check-ins into account introduces more incidental patterns (i.e., noise) than actually useful patterns.

- **Last call of a sequence.** Given a call sequence $c_1().c_2()\ldots c_n()$ included as part of a repository change, we only take the final call $c_n()$ into consideration. This is due to the fact that in Java code, a sequence of "accessor" methods is common and typically only the last call mutates the program environment. Calls like

    ResourcesPlugin.getPlugin().getLog().log()

in ECLIPSE are quite common and taking intermediate portions of the call into account will contribute to noise in the form of associating the intermediate getter calls. Such patterns are not relevant for our purposes, however, they are well-studied and are best mined from a snapshot of a repository rather than from its history (Michail, 2000, 1999; Rysselberghe and Demeyer, 2004).

- **Ignoring common calls.** To further reduce the amount of noise, we ignore some very common method calls, such as the ones listed in Figure 2.3. In practice, we ignore method calls that were added more than 100 times. These methods tend to get intermingled with real usage patterns, essentially causing noisy, "overgrown" ones to be formed.

Method name	Number of additions
equals	9,054
add	6,986
getString	5,295
size	5,118
get	4,709
toString	4,197
getName	3,576
append	3,524
iterator	3,340
length	3,339

Figure 2.3: The most frequently inserted method calls.

2.2.2.2 Considering Small Patterns Only

Generally, patterns that consist of a large number of methods are created due to noise. Another way to reduce the complexity and the amount of noise is to reduce the scope of mining to *small* patterns only.

We employ a combination of the following two strategies.

- **Fine-grained transactions.** As mentioned in Section 2.2.1, Apriori relies on transactions that group related items together. We generally have a choice between using *coarse-grained* or *fine-grained* transactions. Coarse-grained transactions consist of all method calls added in a single revision. Fine-grained transactions additionally group calls by the access path. In Figure 2.1, the coarse-grained transaction corresponding to revision 1.23 of Baz.java is further subdivided into three fine-grained transactions for objects o3, list, and iter. An advantage of fine-grained transactions is that they are smaller, and thus make mining more efficient. The reason for this is that the runtime heavily depends on the size and number of frequent patterns, which are restricted by the size of transactions. Fine-grained transactions also tend to reduce noise because processing is restricted to a common prefix. However, we may miss patterns containing calls with different prefixes, such as pattern {iterator, hasNext, next} in Figure 2.1.

- **Mining method pairs.** We can reduce the the complexity even further if we mine the revision repository only for method pairs instead of patterns of arbitrary size. This technique has frequently been applied to software evolution analysis and proved successful for finding evolutionary coupling (Gall et al., 1998, 2003; Zimmermann et al., 2003). While very common, method pairs can only express relatively simple usage patterns.

2.2.3   Pattern Ranking

Even when filtering is applied, the Apriori algorithm yields many frequent patterns. However, not all of them turn out to be good usage patterns in practice. Therefore, we use several ranking schemes when presenting the patterns we discovered to the user for review.

2.2.3.1   Standard Ranking Approaches

Mining literature provides a number of standard techniques we use for pattern ranking. Among them are the pattern's (1) support count, (2) confidence, and (3) strength, where the strength of a pattern is defined as following.

Definition 2.6 (Strength)
The strength *of pattern p is the number of strong association rules in R of the form $p - q \Rightarrow q$ where $q \subset p$, both p and q are frequent patterns, and $q \neq \emptyset$.*

For our experiments, we rank patterns lexicographically by their strength and support count. However, for matching method pairs $\langle a, b \rangle$ we use the product of confidence values $conf(a \Rightarrow b) \times conf(b \Rightarrow a)$ instead of the strength because the continuous nature of the product gives a more fine-grained ranking than the strength; the strength would only take the values of 0, 1, and 2 for pairs. The advantage of products over sums is that pairs where both confidence values are high are favored. In the rest of the chapter we refer to the ranking that follows classical data mining techniques as *regular ranking*.

2.2.3.2   Corrective Ranking

While the ranking schemes above can generally be applied to any data mining problem, we have come up with a measure of a pattern's importance that is specific to mining revision histories. Observation 2.3 is the basis of the metric we are about to describe. A check-in may only add *parts* of a usage pattern to the repository. Generally, this is a problem for the classic Apriori algorithm, which prefers patterns, where all parts of which are "seen together". However, we can leverage incomplete patterns when we realize that they often represent bug fixes.

A recent study of the dynamic of small repository changes in large software systems performed by Purushothaman et al. sheds a new light on this subject (Purushothaman and Perry, 2005). Their paper points out that almost 50% of all repository changes were small, involving less than 10 lines of code. Moreover, among one-line changes, less than 4% were likely to cause a later error. Furthermore, only less than 2.5% of all one-line changes were *perfective* changes that add functionality, rather than *corrective* changes that correct previous errors. These numbers imply a very strong correlation between one-line changes and bug corrections or fixes.

We use this observation to develop a *corrective ranking* that extends the ranking that is used in classical data mining. For this, we identify one-line fixes and mark method calls that were added at least once in such a fix as *fixed*. In addition to the measures used by regular ranking, we then additionally rank by the number of fixed methods calls which is used as the first lexicographic category. As discussed in Section 2.4, patterns with a high corrective rank in more dynamic violations than patterns with a high regular rank.

2.2.4   Locating Added Method Calls

In order to speed-up the mining process, we pre-process the revision history extracted from CVS and store this information in a general-purpose database; our techniques are further described by Zimmermann and Weißgerber (2004). The database stores method calls that have been inserted for each revision. To determine the calls inserted between two revisions r_1 and r_2, we build abstract syntax trees (ASTs) for both r_1 and r_2 and compute the set of all calls C_1 and C_2, respectively, by traversing the ASTs. $C_2 - C_1$ is the set of inserted calls between r_1 and r_2.

Unlike Williams and Hollingsworth (2005a,b) our approach does not build snapshots of a system. As they point out such interactions with the build environment (compilers, makefiles) are extremely difficult to handle and result in high computational costs. Instead we analyze only the differences between single revisions. As a result our preprocessing is cheap and platform- and compiler-independent; the drawback is that types cannot be resolved because only one file is investigated. In order to avoid noise that is caused by this, we additionally identify methods by the count of arguments. However, if resolved types names are needed they could be generated with a simple search within one program snapshot.

2.3   Checking Patterns at Runtime

In this section we describe our dynamic approach for checking the patterns discovered through revision history mining.

2.3.1   Pattern Selection and Instrumentation

To aid with the task of choosing the relevant patterns, the user is presented with a list of mined patterns in an ECLIPSE view. The list of patterns may be sorted and filtered based on various ranking criteria described in Section 2.2.3 to better target user efforts. Human involvement at this stage, however, is optional, because the user may decide to dynamically check *all* the patterns discovered through revision history mining.

After the user selects the patterns of interest, the list of relevant methods for each of the patterns is generated and passed to the instrumenter. We use JBoss AOP (Burke and Brock, 2003), an aspect-oriented framework to insert additional "bookkeeping" code at the method calls relevant for the patterns. However, the task of pointcut selection is simplified for the user by using a graphical interface. In addition to the method being called and the place in the code where the call occurs, values of all actual parameters are also recorded.

2.3.2   Post-processing Dynamic Traces

The trace produced in the course of a dynamic run are post-processed to produce the final statistics about the number of times each pattern is followed and the number of times it is violated. We decided in favor of off-line post-processing because some patterns are rather difficult and sometimes impossible to match with a fully online approach. In order to facilitate the task of post-processing in practice, DYNAMINE is equipped with checkers to look for matching method pairs and state machines. Users who wish to create checkers for more complex patterns can do so through a Java API exposed by DYNAMINE that allows easy access to runtime events.

Dynamically obtained results for matching pairs and state machines are exported back into ECLIPSE for review. The user can browse through the results and ascertain which of the patterns she thought must hold do actually hold at runtime. Often, examining the dynamic output of DYNAMINE allows the user to correct the initial pattern and re-instrument.

2.3.2.1 Dynamic Interpretation of Patterns

While it may be intuitively obvious what a given coding pattern means, what kind of *dynamic behavior* is valid may be open to interpretation, as illustrated by the following example. Consider a matching method pair ⟨beginOp, endOp⟩ and a dynamic call sequence

$$seq = \text{o.beginOp}() \dots \text{o.beginOp}() \dots \text{o.endOp}().$$

Obviously, a dynamic execution of a sequence of calls o.beginOp() ... o.endOp() follows the pattern. However, execution sequence *seq* probably represents a pattern violation.

While declaring *seq* a violation may appear quite reasonable on the surface, consider now an implementation of method beginOp that starts by calling super.beginOp(). Now *seq* is the dynamic call sequence that results from a static call to o.beginOp followed by o.endOp; the first call to beginOp comes from the static call to beginOp and the second comes from the call to super. However, in this case *seq* may be a completely reasonable interpretation of this coding pattern.

As this example shows, there is generally no obvious mapping from a coding pattern to a dynamic sequence of events. As a result, the number of dynamic pattern matches and mismatches is interpretation-dependent. Errors found by DYNAMINE at runtime can only be considered such with respect to a particular dynamic interpretation of patterns. Moreover, while violations of application-specific patterns found with our approach represent *likely* bugs, they cannot be claimed as definite bugs without carefully studying the effect of each violation on the system.

In the implementation of DYNAMINE, to calculate the number of times each pattern is validated and violated we match the unqualified names of methods applied to a given dynamic object. Fortunately, complete information about the object involved is available at runtime, thus making this sort of matching possible. For patterns that involve only one object, we do not consider method arguments when performing a match: our goal is to have a dynamic matcher that is as automatic as possible for a given type of pattern, and it is not always possible to automatically determine which arguments have to match for a given method pair. For complex patterns that involve more than one object and require user-defined checkers, the trace data saved by DYNAMINE contains information allows the relevant call arguments to be matched.

2.3.2.2 Dynamic vs Static Counts

A single pattern violation at runtime involves one or more objects. We obtain a *dynamic count* by counting how many object combinations participated in a particular pattern violation during program execution. Dynamic counts are highly dependent on how we use the program at runtime and can be easily influenced by, for example, recompiling a project in ECLIPSE multiple times.

Moreover, dynamic error counts are not representative of the work a developer has to do to fix an error, as many dynamic violations can be caused by the same error in the code. To provide a better metric on the number of errors found in the application code, we also compute a *static count*. This is done by mapping each method participating in a pattern to a static call site and counting the number of unique call site combinations that are seen at runtime. Static counts are computed for validated and violated patterns.

2.3.2.3 Pattern Classification

We use runtime information on how many times each pattern is validated and how many times it is violated to classify the patterns. Let v be the number of validated instances of a pattern and e be the number of its violations. The constants used in the classification strategy below were obtained empirically to match our intuition about how patterns should be categorized. However, clearly, ours is but one of many potential classification approaches.

We define an error threshold $\alpha = min(v/10, 100)$. Based on the value of α, patterns can be classified into the following categories:

- **Likely usage patterns**: patterns with a sufficiently high support that are mostly validated with relatively few errors ($e < \alpha \wedge v > 5$).

- **Likely error patterns**: patterns that have a significant number of validated cases as well as a large number of violations ($\alpha \leq e \leq 2v \wedge v > 5$).

- **Unlikely patterns**: patterns that do not have many validated cases or cause too many errors to be usage patterns ($e > 2v \vee v \leq 5$).

2.4 Experimental Results

In this section we discuss our practical experience of applying DYNAMINE to real software systems. Section 2.4.1 describes our experimental setup; Section 2.4.2 evaluates the results of both our patterns mining and dynamic analysis approaches.

2.4.1 Experimental Setup

We performed our experiments on ECLIPSE (Carlson, 2005) and JEDIT (Pestov, 2007), two very large open-source Java applications; in fact, ECLIPSE is one of the largest Java projects ever created. A summary of information about the benchmarks is given in Figure 2.4. For each application, the number of lines of code, source files, and classes is shown in Row 2–4. Both applications are known for being highly extensible and having a large number of plugins available; in fact, much of ECLIPSE itself is implemented as a set of plugins.

In addition to these standard metrics that reflect the size of the benchmarks, we show the number of revisions in each CVS repository in Row 5, the number of inserted calls in Row 6, and the number of distinct methods that were called in Row 7. Both projects have a significant number of individual developers working on them, as evidenced by the numbers in Row 8. The date of the first revision is presented in Row 9.

2.4.1.1 Mining Setup

When we performed the pre-processing on ECLIPSE and JEDIT, it took about four days to fetch all revisions over the Internet because the complete revision data is about 6GB in size and the CVS protocol is not well-suited for retrieving large volumes of history

	ECLIPSE	JEDIT
Lines of code	2,924,124	714,715
Source files	19,115	3,163
Java classes	19,439	6,602
CVS revisions	2,837,854	144,495
Method calls inserted	465,915	56,794
Unique methods called in inserts	59,929	10,760
Developers checking into CVS	122	92
CVS history since	2001-05-02	2000-01-15

Figure 2.4: Summary statistics about the evaluation subjects.

data. Computing inserted methods by analyzing the ASTs and storing this information in a database takes about a day on a Powermac G5 2.3 Ghz dual-processor machine with 1 GB of memory.

Once the pre-processing step was complete, we performed the actual data mining. Without any of the optimizations described in Sections 2.2.2 and 2.2.3, the mining step does not complete even in the case JEDIT, not to mention ECLIPSE. Among the optimizations we apply, the biggest time improvement and noise reduction is achieved by disregarding common method calls, such as `equals`, `length`, etc. With *all* the optimizations applied, mining becomes orders of magnitude faster, usually only taking several minutes.

2.4.1.2 Dynamic Setup

Because the incremental cost of checking for additional patterns at runtime is generally low, when reviewing the patterns in ECLIPSE for inclusion in our dynamic experiments, we were fairly liberal in our selection. We would usually either just look at the method names involved in the pattern or briefly examine a few usage cases. We believe that this strategy is realistic, as we cannot expect the user to spend hours pouring over the patterns. To obtain dynamic results, we ran each application for several minutes on a Pentium 4 machine running Linux, which typically resulted in several thousand dynamic events being generated.

2.4.2   Discussion of the Results

Overall, 32 out of 56 (or 57%) patterns that we selected as interesting were hit at runtime. Furthermore, 21 out of 32 (or 66%) of these patterns turned out to be either usage or error patterns. The fact that two thirds of all dynamically encountered patterns were likely usage or error patterns demonstrates the power of our mining approach. In this section we discuss the categories of patterns briefly introduced in Section 2.1 in more detail.

2.4.2.1   Matching Method Pairs

The simplest and most common kind of a pattern detected with our mining approach is one where two different methods of the same class are supposed to match precisely in execution. Many of known error patterns in the literature such as ⟨fopen, fclose⟩ or ⟨lock, unlock⟩ fall into the category of function calls that require exact matching: failing to call the second function in the pair or calling one of the functions twice in a row is an error.

Figure 2.5 and 2.6 list matching pairs of methods discovered with our mining technique. The methods of a pair ⟨a, b⟩ are listed in the order they are supposed to be executed, e.g., a should be executed before b. For brevity, we only list the names of the method; full method names that include package names should be easy to obtain. A quick glance at the table reveals that many pairs follow a specific naming strategy such as pre-post, add-remove, begin-end, and enter-exit. These pairs could have been discovered by simply pattern matching on the method names. Moreover, looking at method pairs that use the same prefixes or suffixes is an obvious extension of our technique.

However, a significant number of pairs have less than obvious names to look for, including ⟨HLock, HUnlock⟩, ⟨progressStart, progressEnd⟩, and ⟨blockSignal, unblockSignal⟩. Finally, some pairs are very difficult to recognize as matching method pairs and require a detailed study of the API to confirm, e.g., ⟨stopMeasuring, commitMeasurements⟩ or ⟨suspend, resume⟩.

Figure 2.5 and 2.6 summarize dynamic results for matching pairs. The tables provides dynamic and static counts of validated and violated patterns as well as a classification into usage, error, and unlikely patterns. Below we summarize some observations about the data. About a half of all method pair patterns that we selected from the filtered mined results were confirmed as likely patterns, out of those 5 were usage patterns and 9

	METHOD PAIR $\langle a, b \rangle$		CONFIDENCE			SUPPORT	DYNAMIC		STATIC		TYPE
	Method a	Method b	$conf$	$conf_{ab}$	$conf_{ba}$	$count$	v	e	v	e	
			CORRECTIVE RANKING								
ECLIPSE (16 pairs)	NewRgn	DisposeRgn	0.76	0.92	0.82	49			4	1	Unlikely
	kEventControlActivate	kEventControlDeactivate	0.69	0.83	0.83	5			41	28	Unlikely
	addDebugEventListener	removeDebugEventListener	0.61	0.85	0.72	23	4		4	0	Usage
	beginTask	done	0.60	0.74	0.81	493	332	759			
	beginRule	endRule	0.60	0.80	0.74	32	7	0	4		
	suspend	resume	0.60	0.83	0.71	5					
	NewPtr	DisposePtr	0.57	0.82	0.70	23					
	addListener	removeListener	0.57	0.68	0.83	90	143	140	35	29	Error
	register	deregister	0.54	0.69	0.78	40	2,854	461	17	90	Error
	malloc	free	0.47	0.68	0.68	28					
	addElementChangedListener	removeElementChangedListener	0.42	0.73	0.57	8	6	1	1	1	Error
	addResourceChangeListener	removeResourceChangeListener	0.41	0.90	0.46	26	27	1	21	1	Usage
	addPropertyChangeListener	removePropertyChangeListener	0.40	0.54	0.73	140	1,864	309	54	31	Error
	start	stop	0.39	0.59	0.65	32	69	18	20	9	Error
	addDocumentListener	removeDocumentListener	0.36	0.64	0.56	29	38	2	14	2	Usage
	addSyncSetChangedListener	removeSyncSetChangedListener	0.34	0.62	0.56	24					
JEDIT (8 pairs)	addNotify	removeNotify	0.60	0.77	0.77	17	3	0	3	0	Unlikely
	setBackground	setForeground	0.57	0.67	0.86	12	75	175	5	5	Unlikely
	contentRemoved	contentInserted	0.51	0.71	0.71	5	17	11	7	5	Error
	setInitialDelay	start	0.40	0.80	0.50	4	0	32	0	2	Unlikely
	registerErrorSource	unregisterErrorSource	0.28	0.45	0.62	5					
	start	stop	0.20	0.39	0.52	33	83	98	10	13	Error
	addToolBar	removeToolBar	0.18	0.60	0.30	6	24	43	5	5	Error
	init	save	0.09	0.40	0.24	31					
(24 pairs)	Subtotals for the corrective ranking scheme:						5,546	2,051	245	222	3 U, 8 E
(52 pairs)	Overall totals (includes both corrective and regular ranking):						16,901	2,298	254	241	10 U, 8 E

Figure 2.5: Matching method pairs discovered through CVS history mining (**corrective ranking**). The support count is $count$, the confidence for $\{a\} \Rightarrow \{b\}$ is $conf_{ab}$, for $\{b\} \Rightarrow \{a\}$ it is $conf_{ba}$. The pairs are ordered by $conf = conf_{ab} \times conf_{ba}$. In the last column, usage and error patterns are abbreviated as "U" and "E", respectively. Empty cells represent patterns that have not been observed at runtime.

Figure 2.6: Matching method pairs discovered through CVS history mining (**regular ranking**). The support count is $count$, the confidence for $\{a\} \Rightarrow \{b\}$ is $conf_{ab}$, for $\{b\} \Rightarrow \{a\}$ it is $conf_{ba}$. The pairs are ordered by $conf = conf_{ab} \times conf_{ba}$. In the last column, usage and error patterns are abbreviated as "U" and "E", respectively. Empty cells represent patterns that have not been observed at runtime.

METHOD PAIR ⟨a,b⟩		CONFIDENCE			SUPPORT	DYNAMIC		STATIC		TYPE
Method a	**Method b**	conf	$conf_{ab}$	$conf_{ba}$	count	v	e	v	e	
ECLIPSE (15 pairs)			REGULAR RANKING							
createPropertyList	reapPropertyList	1.00	1.00	1.00	174	40	0	26	0	Usage
preReplaceChild	postReplaceChild	1.00	1.00	1.00	133					
preLazyInit	postLazyInit	1.00	1.00	1.00	112					
preValueChange	postValueChange	1.00	1.00	1.00	46	63	2	11	2	Usage
addWidget	removeWidget	1.00	1.00	1.00	35	2,507	16	26	6	Usage
stopMeasuring	commitMeasurements	1.00	1.00	1.00	15					
blockSignal	unblockSignal	1.00	1.00	1.00	13					
Hlock	HUnlock	1.00	1.00	1.00	9					
addInputChangedListener	removeInputChangedListener	1.00	1.00	1.00	9					
preRemoveChildEvent	postAddChildEvent	1.00	1.00	1.00	8	0	171	0	3	Unlikely
progressStart	progressEnd	1.00	1.00	1.00	8					
CGContextSaveGState	CGContextRestoreGState	1.00	1.00	1.00	7					
addInsert	addDelete	1.00	1.00	1.00	7					
annotationAdded	annotationRemoved	1.00	1.00	1.00	7	0	10	0	4	Unlikely
OpenEvent	fireOpen	1.00	1.00	1.00	7	3	0	1	0	Unlikely
JEDIT (13 pairs)										
readLock	readUnlock	1.00	1.00	1.00	16	8,578	0	14	0	Usage
setHandler	parse	1.00	1.00	1.00	6	12	0	8	0	Usage
addTo	removeFrom	1.00	1.00	1.00	5					
execProcess	ssCommand	1.00	1.00	1.00	4					
freeMemory	totalMemory	1.00	1.00	1.00	4	95	0	2	0	Usage
lockBuffer	unlockBuffer	1.00	1.00	1.00	4					
writeLock	writeUnlock	0.85	1.00	0.85	11	38	0	8	0	Usage
allocConnection	releaseConnection	0.83	1.00	0.83	5					
getSubregionOfOffset	xToSubregionOffset	0.80	0.80	1.00	4					
initTextArea	uninitTextArea	0.80	0.80	1.00	4					
undo	redo	0.69	0.83	0.83	5	0	4	0	1	Unlikely
setSelectedItem	getSelectedItem	0.37	0.50	0.73	11	7	17	7	7	Unlikely
addToSelection	setSelection	0.29	0.57	0.50	4	12	27	1	9	Unlikely
(28 pairs)		Subtotals for the regular ranking scheme:				11,355	247	104	32	7 U
(52 pairs)		Overall totals (includes both corrective and regular ranking):				16,901	2,298	245	254	10 U, 8 E

were error patterns. Many more potentially interesting matching pairs become available if we consider lower support counts; for the experiments we have only considered patterns with a support of four or more.

Several characteristic pairs are described below. The JEDIT locking pairs ⟨writeLock, writeUnlock⟩ and ⟨readLock, readUnlock⟩ are excellent usage patterns with no violations. The pair ⟨contentInserted, contentRemoved⟩ is not a good pattern despite the method names: the first method is triggered when text is added in an editor window; the second when text is removed. Clearly, there is no reason why these two methods have to match. Method pair ⟨addNotify, removeNotify⟩ is perfectly matched, however, its support is not sufficient to declare it a usage pattern. An unusual kind of matching methods that at first we thought was caused by noise in the data consists of a constructor call followed by a method call, such as the pair ⟨OpenEvent, fireOpen⟩. This sort of pattern indicates that all objects of type OpenEvent should be "consumed" by passing them into method fireOpen. Violations of this pattern may lead to resource and memory leaks, a serious problem in long-running Java programs such as ECLIPSE, which may be open at a developer's desktop for days.

Overall, corrective ranking was significantly more effective than the regular ranking schemes that are based on the product of confidence values. The top half of the table that addresses patterns obtained with corrective ranking contains 24 matching method pairs; the second half that deals with the patterns obtained with regular ranking contains 28 pairs. Looking at the subtotals for each ranking scheme reveals 241 static validating instances vs. only 104 for regular ranking; 222 static error instances are found vs. only 32 for regular ranking. Finally, 11 pairs found with corrective ranking were dynamically confirmed as either error or usage patterns vs. 7 for regular ranking. This confirms our belief that corrective ranking is more effective.

2.4.2.2 State Machines

In many of cases, the order in which methods are supposed to be called *on a given object* can easily be captured with a finite state machine. Typically, such state machines must be followed precisely: omitting or repeating a method call is a sign of error. The fact that state machines are encountered often is not surprising: state machines are the simplest formalism for describing the object life-cycle (Schach, 2004). Matching method pairs are a specific case of state machines, but there are other prominent cases that involve *more that two methods*, which are the focus of this section.

An example of state machine usage comes from the class `Scribe` in ECLIPSE (from the package `org.eclipse.jdt.internal.formatter`), which is responsible for pretty-printing Java source code. The method `exitAlignment` is supposed to match an earlier `enterAlignment` call to preserve consistency. Typically, method `redoAlignment` that tries to resolve an exception caused by the current `enterAlignment` would be placed in a `catch` block and executed optionally, only if an exception is raised. The regular expression

$$o.\texttt{enterAlignment } o.\texttt{redoAlignment? } o.\texttt{exitAlignment}$$

summarizes how methods of this class are supposed to be called on an object o of type `Scribe`. In our dynamic experiments, the pattern matched 885 times with only 17 dynamic violations that correspond to 9 static violations, which makes this an excellent usage pattern.

Another interesting state machine below is found based on mining JEDIT. The two methods `beginCompoundEdit` and `endCompoundEdit` are used to group editing operations on a text buffer together so that undo or redo actions can be later applied to them at once.

$$o.\texttt{beginCompoundEdit}()$$
$$(o.\texttt{insert}(...) \mid o.\texttt{remove}(...))^{+}$$
$$o.\texttt{endCompoundEdit}()$$

A dynamic study of this pattern reveals that (1) the two methods `beginCompoundEdit` and `endCompoundEdit` are *perfectly* matched in all cases; (2) 86% of calls to `insert`/`remove` are *within* a compound edit; (3) there are three cases of several ⟨begin−, endCompoundEdit⟩ pairs that have no `insert` or `remove` operations between them. Since a compound edit is established for a reason, this shows that our regular expression most likely does not fully describe the life-cycle of a `Buffer` object. Indeed, a detailed study of the code reveals some other methods that may be used within a compound edit. Subsequently adding these methods to the pattern and re-instrumenting the JEDIT led to a pattern that fully describes the `Buffer` object's life-cycle.

Precisely following the order in which methods must be called is common for C interfaces (Engler et al., 2000), as represented by functions that manipulate files and sockets. While such dependency on call order is less common in Java, it still occurs in programs that have low-level access to OS data structures. For instance, methods `PmMemCreateMC`, `PmMemFlush`, and `PmMemStop`, `PmMemReleaseMC` declared in `org.eclipse.swt.OS` in ECLIPSE expose low-level memory context management routines in Java through the use of JNI wrappers. These methods are supposed to be called in order described by the regular expression below:

OS.PmMemCreateMC
　　(OS.PmMemStart OS.PmMemFlush OS.PmMemStop)?
OS.PmMemReleaseMC

The first and last lines are mandatory when using this pattern, while the middle line is optional. Unfortunately, this pattern only exhibits itself at runtime on certain platforms, so we were unable to confirm it dynamically.

Another similar JNI wrapper found in ECLIPSE that can be expressed as a state machine is responsible for region-based memory allocation and can be described with the following regular expression:

(OS.NewPtr | OS.NewPtrClear) OS.DisposePtr

Either one of functions NewPtr and NewPtrClear can be used to create a new pointer; the latter function zeroes-out the memory region before returning.

The hierarchical allocation of resources is another common usage pattern that can be captured with a state machine. Objects request and release system resources in a way that is perfectly nested. For instance, one of the patterns we found in ECLIPSE suggests the following resource management scheme on objects of type component:

o.createHandle() o.register()
　　　　　o.deregister() o.releaseHandle()

The call to createHandle requests an operating system resource for a GUI widget, such as a window or a button; releaseHandle frees this OS resource for subsequent use. register associates the current GUI object with a display data structure, which is responsible for forwarding GUI events to components as they arrive; deregister breaks this link.

2.4.2.3 More Complex Patterns

More complicated patterns, that are concerned with the behavior of more than one object or patterns for which a finite state machine is not expressive enough, are quite widespread in the code base we have considered as well. Notice that approaches that use a restrictive model of a pattern such as matching function calls (Engler et al., 2001), would not be able to find these complex patterns.

```
try {
  monitor.beginTask(null, Policy.totalWork);
  int depth = -1;
  try {
      workspace.prepareOperation(null, monitor);
      workspace.beginOperation(true);
      depth = workspace.getWorkManager().beginUnprotected();
      return runInWorkspace(Policy.subMonitorFor(monitor,
          Policy.opWork,
          SubProgressMonitor.PREPEND_MAIN_LABEL_TO_SUBTASK));
  } catch (OperationCanceledException e) {
      workspace.getWorkManager().operationCanceled();
      return Status.CANCEL_STATUS;
  } finally {
      if (depth >= 0)
          workspace.getWorkManager().endUnprotected(depth);
      workspace.endOperation(null, false,
      Policy.subMonitorFor(monitor, Policy.endOpWork));
  }
} catch (CoreException e) {
    return e.getStatus();
} finally {
    monitor.done();
}
```

Figure 2.7: Example of workspace operations and locking discipline usage in the ECLIPSE class `InternalWorkspaceJob`. Lines pertaining to the pattern are shown in bold.

We only describe one complex pattern in detail here, which is motivated by the the code snippet in Figure 2.7. The lines relevant to the pattern are highlighted in bold. Object `workspace` is a runtime representation of an ECLIPSE workspace, a large complex object that has a specialized transaction scheme for when it needs to be modified. In particular, one is supposed to start the transaction that requires workspace access with a call to `beginOperation` and finish it with `endOperation`.

Calls to `beginUnprotected()` and `endUnprotected()` on a `WorkManager` object obtained from the `workspace` indicate "unlocked" operations: the first call releases the workspace lock that is held by default and the second call re-acquires the lock; the `WorkManager` is obtained for a `workspace` by calling `workspace.getWorkManager`.

Unlocking operations should be precisely matched if no error occurs; in case an exception is raised, the operationCanceled method is called on the WorkManager of the current workspace. As can be seen from the code in Figure 2.7, this pattern involves error handling and may be quite tricky to get right. We have come across this pattern by observing that pairs ⟨beginOperation, endOperation⟩ and ⟨beginUnprotected, endUnprotected⟩ are both highly correlated in the code.

This pattern is easily described as a context-free language that allows nested matching brackets, whose grammar is shown below.[2]

$$
\begin{aligned}
S \;\; &\rightarrow \;\; O^\star \\
O \;\; &\rightarrow \;\; \texttt{w.prepareOperation()} \\
& \qquad \texttt{w.beginOperation()} \\
& \qquad U^\star \\
& \qquad \texttt{w.endOperation()} \\
U \;\; &\rightarrow \;\; \texttt{w.getWorkManager().beginUnprotected()} \\
& \qquad S \\
& \qquad \texttt{w.getWorkManager().operationCanceled() ?} \\
& \qquad \texttt{w.getWorkManager().beginUnprotected()}
\end{aligned}
$$

This is a very strong usage patterns in ECLIPSE, with 100% of the cases we have seen obeying the grammar above. The nesting of Workspace and WorkManager operations was usually 3–4 levels deep in practice.

2.5 Related Work

A vast amount of work has been done in bug detection. C and C++ code in particular is prone to buffer overrun and memory management errors; tools such as PREfix (Bush et al., 2000) and Clouseau (Heine and Lam, 2003) are representative examples of systems designed to find specific classes of bugs (pointer errors and object ownership violations respectively). Dynamic systems include Purify (Hastings and Joyce, 1992), which traps heap errors, and Eraser (Savage et al., 1997), which detects race conditions. Both of these analyses have been implemented as standard uses of the Valgrind system (Nethercote and Seward, 2003).

---

[2]S is the grammar start symbol and * is used to represent 0 or more copies of the preceding non-terminal; ? indicates that the preceding non-terminal is optional.

Much attention has been given to detecting high-profile software defects in important domains such as operating system bugs (Hallem et al., 2002; Heine and Lam, 2003), security bugs (Shankar et al., 2001; Wagner et al., 2000), bugs in firmware (Kumar and Li, 2002) and errors in reliability-critical embedded systems (Blanchet et al., 2003; Brat and Venet, 2005).

Engler et al. (2001) are among the first to point out the need for extracting rules to be used in bug-finding tools. They employ a static analysis approach and statistical techniques to find likely instantiations of pattern templates such as matching function calls. Our mining technique is not a-priori limited to a particular set of pattern templates, however, it is powerless when it comes to patterns that are never added to the repository after the first revision.

Several projects focus on application-specific error patterns, including SABER (Reimer et al., 2004) that deals with J2EE patterns and Metal (Hallem et al., 2002), which addresses bugs in OS code. Certain categories of patterns can be gleaned from AntiPattern literature (Dudney et al., 2003; Tate et al., 2003), although many AntiPatterns tend to deal with high-level architectural concerns than with low-level coding issues.

In the rest of this section, we review literature pertinent to revision history mining and software model extraction.

2.5.1 Revision History Mining

Previous research in the area of mining software repositories investigated the location of a change—such as files (Bevan and Whitehead, Jr., 2003), classes (Bieman et al., 2003; Gall et al., 2003), or methods (Zimmermann et al., 2003)—and properties of changes—such as number of lines changed, developers, or whether a change is a fix (Mockus and Weiss, 2000).

Recently, the focus shifted from locations to changes themselves: Kim et al. (2005) identified signature change patterns in version histories. Fluri and Gall (2006) classified fine-grained changes and Fluri et al. (2007) presented a tool to compare abstract syntax trees to extract fine-grained change informaton. Several other approaches used abstract syntax tree matching to understand software evolution (Neamtiu et al., 2005; Sager et al., 2006). Finding out what was changed is an instance of the program element matching problem that has been surveyed by Kim and Notkin (2006).

Most work on preprocessing version archives covers problems specific to CVS such as mirroring CVS archives, reconstructing transactions, reducing noise and finding out the locations (methods) that changed (Fischer et al., 2003a; Fluri et al., 2005; German, 2004; Zimmermann and Weißgerber, 2004). The Kenyon tool combines these techniques in one framework; it is frequently used for software evolution research (Bevan et al., 2005). For the data processing in this book, we used the APFEL tool, which is based on tokens (Zimmermann, 2006).

One of the most frequently used techniques for revision history mining is co-change. The basic idea is that items that are changed together, are related to one another. These items can be of any granularity; in the past co-change has been applied to changes in modules (Gall et al., 1998), files (Bevan and Whitehead, Jr., 2003), classes (Bieman et al., 2003; Gall et al., 2003), and functions (Zimmermann et al., 2003).

Recent research improves on co-change by applying data mining techniques to revision histories (Ying et al., 2004; Zimmermann et al., 2005). Michail (2000, 1999) used data mining on the source code of programming libraries to detect reuse patterns, but not for revision histories only for single snapshots. Our work is the first to apply co-change and data mining based on method calls. While Fischer et al. (2003b) were the first to combine bug databases with dynamic analysis, our work is the first that combines the mining of revision histories with dynamic analysis.

The work most closely related to ours is that by Williams and Hollingsworth (2005b). They were the first to combine program analysis and revision history mining. Their paper proposes error ranking improvements for a static return value checker with information about fixes obtained from revision histories. Our work differs from theirs in several important ways: they focus on prioritizing or improving existing error patterns and checkers, whereas we concentrate on discovering new ones. Furthermore, we use dynamic analysis and thus do not face high false positive rates their tool suffers from. Recently, Williams and Hollingsworth (2005a) also turned towards mining function usage patterns from revision histories. In contrast to our work, they focus only on pairs and do not use their patterns to detect violations.

2.5.2 Model Extraction

Most work on automatically inferring state models on components of software systems has been done using dynamic analysis techniques.

The Strauss system (Ammons et al., 2002) uses machine learning techniques to infer a state machine representing the proper sequence of function calls in an interface. Dallmeier et al. (2005) trace call sequences and correlate sequence patterns with test failures. Whaley et al. (2002) hardcode a restricted model paradigm so that probable models of object-oriented interfaces can be easily automatically extracted. Alur et al. (2005) generalize this to automatically produce small, expressive finite state machines with respect to certain predicates over an object.

Lam and Rinard (2003) use a type system-based approach to statically extract interfaces. Their work is more concerned with high-level system structure rather than low-level life-cycle constraints (Schach, 2004). Daikon is able to validate correlations between values at runtime and is therefore able to validate patterns (Ernst et al., 2001). Weimer and Necula (2005) use exception control flow paths to guide the discovery of temporal error patterns with considerable success; they also provide a comparison with other existing specification mining work.

2.6 Summary

In this chapter, we presented DYNAMINE, a tool for learning common usage patterns from the revision histories of large software systems. Our method can learn both simple and complicated patterns, scales to millions of lines of code, and has been used to find more than 250 pattern violations. Our mining approach is effective at finding coding patterns: two thirds of all dynamically encountered patterns turned out to be likely patterns.

DYNAMINE is the first tool that combines revision history information with dynamic analysis for the purpose of finding software errors. Our tool largely automates the mining and dynamic execution steps and makes the results of both steps more accessible by presenting the discovered patterns as well as the results of dynamic checking to the user in custom ECLIPSE views.

Optimization and filtering strategies that we developed allowed us to reduce the mining time by orders of magnitude and to find high-quality patterns in millions lines of code in a matter of minutes. Our ranking strategy that favored patterns with previous bug fixes proved to be very effective at finding error patterns. In contrast, classical ranking schemes from data mining could only locate usage patterns. Dynamic analysis proved invaluable in establishing trust in patterns and finding their violations.

3

Mining Aspects from Version History

As object-oriented programs evolve over time, they may suffer from *"the tyranny of dominant decomposition"* (Tarr et al., 1999): They can be modularized in only one way at a time. Concerns that are added later may no longer align with that modularization, and thus, end up scattered across many modules and tangled with one another. Aspect-oriented programming (AOP) remedies this by factoring out aspects and weaving them back in a separate processing step (Kiczales et al., 1997). For existing projects to benefit from AOP, these cross-cutting concerns must be identified first. This task is called *aspect mining*.

We solve this problem by taking a historical perspective: we mine the history of a project and identify code changes that are likely to be cross-cutting concerns; we call them *aspect candidates*. Our analysis is based on the hypothesis that cross-cutting concerns evolve within a project over time. A code change is likely to introduce such a concern if the modification gets introduced at various locations within a single code change.

Our hypothesis is supported by the following example. On November 10, 2004, Silenio Quarti committed code changes "76595 (new lock)" to the ECLIPSE CVS repository. They fixed bug #76595 "Hang in gfk_pixbuf_new" that reported a deadlock and

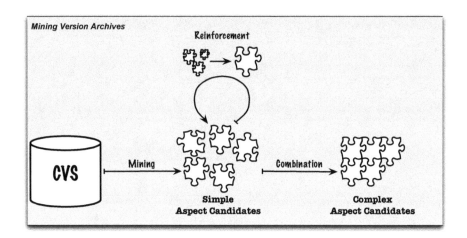

Figure 3.1: Mining cross-cutting concerns with HAM.

required the implementation of a new locking mechanism for several platforms. The extent of the modification was enormous: He modified 2,573 methods and inserted in 1,284 methods a call to lock, as well as a call to unlock. As it turns out, AOP could have been used to add these.

Our approach searches such cross-cutting changes in the history of a program in order to identify aspect candidates. For Silenio Quarti's changes, we find two *simple aspect candidates* ($\{\texttt{lock}\}, L_1$) and ($\{\texttt{unlock}\}, L_2$) where L_1 and L_2 are sets that contain the 1,284 methods where lock and unlock have been inserted, respectively. It turns out that $L_1 = L_2$, hence, we combine the two aspect candidates into one *complex aspect candidate* ($\{\texttt{lock}, \texttt{unlock}\}, L_1$).

Technically, we mine version archives for aspect candidates (see Figure 3.1). Our implementation HAM first identifies simple aspect candidates in transactions (Section 3.1). Next, we combine simple aspect candidates into complex ones that consider more than one method call (Section 3.3). We may get several aspect candidates for the same cross-cutting concern when it was added in several transactions. *Reinforcement* combines such candidates by exploiting *localities* between transactions (Section 3.2).

We evaluated HAM with three open-source JAVA projects: JHotDraw (57,360 LOC), Columba (103,094 LOC), and ECLIPSE (1,675,025 LOC). For each project we ranked candidates and validated the top-50 candidates manually. Our results are promising: the average precision is around 50% with the best values for ECLIPSE; for the top-10 candidates in ECLIPSE, HAM's precision is better than 90% (Section 3.5).

3.1   Simple Aspect Candidates

Previous approaches to aspect mining considered only a single version of a program using static and dynamic program analysis techniques. Our approach introduces an additional dimension: the *history* of a project.

We model the history of a program as a sequence of transactions. A *transaction* collects all code changes between two versions, called *snapshots*, made by a programmer to complete a single development task. Technically a transaction is defined by the version archive we analyze, which is CVS in our case. However, our approach extends to arbitrary version archives.

Motivated by dynamic approaches for aspect mining that investigate execution traces of programs, we build our analysis on changes that insert or delete method calls. Typically, these changes have direct impact on execution traces. But since we are looking for the introduction of cross-cutting concerns, we concentrate solely on additions and omit deletions of method calls. This means that for our purpose a transaction consists of the set of method calls that were inserted by a developer.

Definition 3.1 (Transaction)
A transaction T is a set of pairs (m, l). Each pair (m, l) represents an insertion of a call to method m in the body of the method l.

We name the method l into which a call is inserted *method location* and identify it by its full signature. In contrast, to reduce the cost of preprocessing, we identify the called method m only by its name and number of arguments (see Section 3.4). We associate the following meta-data with a transaction T:

1. *developer*(T) is the name of developer who committed transaction T.

2. *timestamp*(T) is when a transaction T was committed.

3. *locations*$(T) = \{l \mid (m, l) \in T\}$ is the set of methods that were changed in transaction T.

4. *calls*$(T) = \{m \mid (m, l) \in T\}$ is the set of method calls that were added in transaction T.

Algorithm 3.1 Simple aspect candidates

 1: **function** CANDIDATES(T)
 2:     $C_{result} = \emptyset$
 3:     **for all** $m \in calls(T)$ **do**
 4:         $L = \{l \mid l \in locations(T), (m, l) \in T\}$
 5:         $C_{result} = C_{result} \cup \{(m, L)\}$
 6:     **end for**
 7:     **return** C_{result}
 8: **end function**
 9:
10: **function** SIMPLE_CANDIDATES($\mathcal{T}$)
11:     **return** $\bigcup_{T \in \mathcal{T}}$ CANDIDATES(T)
12: **end function**

Within the set $\mathcal{T}$ of transactions we are searching for *aspect candidates*. An aspect candidate represents a cross-cutting concern in the sense that it consists of one or more calls to methods M that are spread across several method locations L.

Definition 3.2 (Aspect Candidate)
An aspect candidate $c = (M, L)$ consists of a non-empty set M of methods and a non-empty set L of locations where each location $l \in L$ calls each method $m \in M$. If $|M| = 1$, the aspect candidate c is called simple*; if $|M| > 1$, it is called* complex.

Basically every method call m added in transaction T leads to a potential aspect candidate. Algorithm 3.1 reflects this idea in function SIMPLE_CANDIDATES($\mathcal{T}$) which returns for every transaction $T \in \mathcal{T}$ and every method call $m \in calls(T)$ one aspect candidate. The result would be huge for projects like ECLIPSE with many method calls and a long history. Thus, we use filtering and ranking to find actual aspect candidates.

In order to identify aspect candidates that actually cross-cut a considerable part of a program, we ignore all candidates $c = (M, L)$ where less than eight locations are cross-cut, i.e., $|L| < 8$. Thus, we get large, homogeneous cross-cutting concerns. We focus on them as maintenance will benefit most from their modularization in aspects. We chose the cut-off value of eight based on our previous experience (Livshits and Zimmermann, 2005); for some projects lower cut-off values may be required. In addition to filtering, we use the following ranking techniques:

Rank by Size. Obviously, candidates that cross-cut many locations could be more interesting. Thus, we sort aspect candidates $c = (M, L)$ by their size $|L|$ (from large to small). However, we may get noise in form of method calls that are frequent in JAVA but are not cross-cutting, e.g., iter(), hasNext(), or next().

Rank by Fragmentation. This ranking penalizes calls to common JAVA methods when they appear in many transactions. If a cross-cutting concern is added to a system and not changed later on, it appears in only one transaction. To capture such aspects, we sort aspect candidates by the number of transactions in which we find a candidate (fewer is better). We term this count the *fragmentation* of an aspect candidate $c = (M, L)$:

$$fragmentation(c) = |\{T \in \mathcal{T} \mid M \subseteq calls(T)\}|$$

In case aspect candidates have the same fragmentation because they occur in the same number of transactions, we rank additionally by size $|L|$.

Rank by Compactness. Similar to the ranking by fragmentation, this ranking has the advantage that common JAVA method calls are ranked low. Cross-cutting concerns may be introduced in one transaction and extended to additional locations in later transactions. Since such concerns will be ranked low with the previous rankings, we use *compactness* as a third ranking technique (from high to low). The compactness of an aspect candidate $c = (M, L)$ is the ratio between the size $|L|$ and the total number of locations where calls to M occurred in the history:

$$compactness(c) = \frac{|L|}{|\{l \mid \exists T \in \mathcal{T}, \forall m \in M : (m, l) \in T\}|}$$

In the case that two or more aspect candidates have the same compactness, we rank additionally by size $|L|$.

3.2 Locality and Reinforcement

In our experiments, we observed that several cross-cutting concerns were introduced within one transaction and later extended to other locations. This can happen because a developer introduces changes per package and submits each modified package right

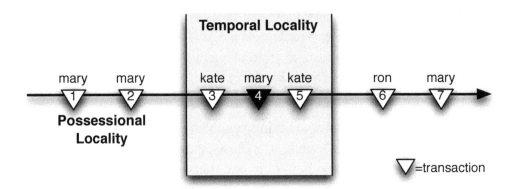

Figure 3.2: Possessional and temporal locality for transaction 4.

away before proceeding to the next, or because he forgot to modify a few places and fixes it in a later transaction to the CVS. This happens frequently when a developer recognizes he must complete a task that he had left unfinished with his last commit. Although such concerns are recognized by our technique as multiple aspect candidates, these candidates may be ranked low and missed.

To strengthen aspect candidates that were inserted in several transactions, we use the concept of *locality*. Two transactions are locally related if they were created by the same developer or were committed around the same time. If there exists locality between transactions, we *reinforce* their aspect candidates mutually.

- **Temporal Locality** refers to the fact that aspect candidates may appear in several transactions that are close in time. In Figure 3.2 there exists temporal locality between transaction 4 and transactions 3 and 5.

- **Possessional Locality** refers to the fact that aspect candidates may have been created by one developer but committed in different transactions; thus they are *owned* by her. Gîrba et al. (2005) define ownership by the last change to a line; in contrast, we look for the addition of method calls, which is more fine-grained. In Figure 3.2 there exists possessional locality between transaction 4 and transactions 1, 2, and 7, all of them were committed by Mary.

Definition 3.3 (Locality)
Let $T_1, T_1 \in \mathcal{T}$ be arbitrary transactions, $c = (M, L)$ be an aspect candidate, and t be a fixed time interval. We say T_1 and T_2 have

1. temporal locality, *written as* $T_1 \overset{time}{\longleftrightarrow} T_2$ *iff*

$$|timestamp(T_1) - timestamp(T_2)| \leq t$$

2. possessional locality, *written as* $T_1 \overset{dev}{\longleftrightarrow} T_2$ *iff*

$$developer(T_1) = developer(T_2)$$

Presume that we found two aspect candidates $c_1 = (M_1, L_1)$ and $c_2 = (M_2, L_2)$ in two different transactions where the called methods are the same, i.e., $M_1 = M_2$. If there exists locality of either form between these two transactions, we can combine both aspect candidates. As a result we get a new aspect candidate $c' = (M_1, L_1 \cup L_2)$. We call this process *reinforcement*.

Definition 3.4 (Reinforcement)
Let $c_1 = (M_1, L_1)$ and $c_2 = (M_2, L_2)$ be aspect candidates. If $M_1 = M_2$, the construction of a new aspect candidate $(M, L_1 \cup L_2)$ with $M = M_1 = M_2$ is called reinforcement.

We implemented three reinforcement algorithms, which are listed in Algorithm 3.2. The functions for temporal (TEMPORAL) and for possessional (POSSESSIONAL) reinforcement both call function REINFORCE which

1. takes a set $\mathcal{T}$ of transactions as input,

2. identifies for each transaction T other transactions $\mathcal{T}_{loc}$ that are related to T with respect to the given locality x,

3. computes for each of these transactions the simple aspect candidates, and

4. builds new combined, or *reinforced* candidates.

Additionally, we implemented an algorithm ALL that combines the results of temporal and possessional reinforcement. However, it does not use the localities at the same time as this could reinforce all transactions and would thereby lose the historic perspective of our approach, but applies them independently.

Algorithm 3.2 Reinforcement algorithms

 1: **function** REINFORCE($\mathcal{T}$, $x \in \{\text{time}, \text{dev}\}$)
 2:     $C_{reinf} = \emptyset$
 3:     **for all** $T \in \mathcal{T}$ **do**
 4:         $\mathcal{T}_{loc} = \left\{ T' \mid T' \in \mathcal{T}, T' \stackrel{x}{\rightsquigarrow} T \right\}$
 5:         $C_{loc} = \bigcup_{T' \in \mathcal{T}_{loc}} \text{CANDIDATES}(T')$
 6:         **for all** $c = (M, L) \in \text{CANDIDATES}(T)$ **do**
 7:             $L_{reinf} = \{ L' \mid c' = (M', L') \in C_{loc}, M' = M \}$
 8:             $C_{reinf} = C_{reinf} \cup \{ (M, L_{reinf}) \}$
 9:         **end for**
10:     **end for**
11:     **return** C_{reinf}
12: **end function**
13:
14: **function** TEMPORAL($\mathcal{T}$)
15:     **return** REINFORCE($\mathcal{T}$, time)
16: **end function**
17:
18: **function** POSSESSIONAL($\mathcal{T}$)
19:     **return** REINFORCE($\mathcal{T}$, dev)
20: **end function**
21:
22: **function** ALL($\mathcal{T}$)
23:     **return** TEMPORAL($\mathcal{T}$) $\cup$ POSSESSIONAL($\mathcal{T}$)
24: **end function**

3.3 Complex Aspect Candidates

Many cross-cutting concerns call more than one method like the lock/unlock concern which we presented at the beginning of Chapter 3. To locate such concerns we combine two aspect candidates $c_1 = (M_1, L_1)$ and $c_2 = (M_2, L_2)$ to a complex aspect candidate $c' = (M', L')$ with $M' = M_1 \cup M_2$ and $L' = L_1$, if c_1 and c_2 cross-cut exactly the same locations, i.e., $L_1 = L_2$. This condition is very selective, however, method calls inserted in the same locations are very likely to be related.

Algorithm 3.3 Complex aspect candidates

1: **function** COMPLEX_CANDIDATES(C_{simple})
2:      $C_{result} = \emptyset$
3:      **for all** $(M, L) \in C_{simple}$ **do**
4:          $\mathcal{M} = \{M' \mid (M', L') \in C_{simple}, L = L'\}$
5:          $M_{complex} = \bigcup_{M' \in \mathcal{M}} M'$
6:          $C_{result} = C_{result} \cup \{(M_{complex}, L)\}$
7:      **end for**
8:      **return** C_{result}
9: **end function**

The function COMPLEX_CANDIDATES in Algorithm 3.3 constructs complex aspect candidates. It takes all simple aspect candidates as input and combines candidates with matching method locations into a new complex aspect candidate. Note that it also combines simple aspect candidates that were inserted in different transactions.

3.4 Data Collection

Our mining approach can be applied to any version control system; however, we based our implementation on CVS since most open-source projects use it. One of the major drawbacks of CVS is that commits are split into individual check-ins and have to be reconstructed. For this we use a *sliding time window* approach (Zimmermann and Weißgerber, 2004) with a 200 seconds window. A reconstructed commit consists of a set of revisions R where each revision $r \in R$ is the result of a single check-in.

Additionally, we need to compute method calls that have been inserted within a commit operation R. For this, we build abstract syntax trees (ASTs) for every revision $r \in R$ and its predecessor and compute the set of all calls C_1 in r and C_0 for the preprocessor by traversing the ASTs. Then $C_r = C_1 - C_0$ is the set of inserted calls within r; the union of all C_r for $r \in R$ forms a *transaction* $T = \bigcup_{r \in R} C_r$ which serves as input for our aspect mining and are stored in a database.

Since we analyze only differences between single revisions, we cannot resolve types because only one file is investigated at a time. In particular, we miss the signature of called methods; to limit noise that is caused by this, we use the number of arguments in addition to method names to identify methods calls. This heuristic is frequently used when analyzing single files (Livshits and Zimmermann, 2005; Xie and Pei, 2006). We would get full method signatures when building *snapshots* of a system. However, as Williams and Hollingsworth (2005b) point out, such interactions with the build environment (compilers, make files) are extremely difficult to handle, require manual interaction, and result in high computational costs. In contrast, our preprocessing is cheap, as well as platform- and compiler-independent.

Renaming of a method is represented as deleting and introducing several method calls. We thus may incidentally consider renamed calls as aspect candidates. Recognizing such changes is known as *origin analysis* (Godfrey and Zou, 2005) and will be implemented in a future version of HAM. It will eliminate some false positives and improve precision.

3.5   Evaluation

In the introduction we told an anecdote how we identified cross-cutting concerns in the history of ECLIPSE. Another example for a cross-cutting concern is the call to method dumpPcNumber which was inserted to 205 methods in the `DefaultBytecodeVisitor` class. This class implements a visitor for bytecode, in particular one method for each bytecode instruction; the following code shows the method for instruction aload_0.

```
/**
 * @see IBytecodeVisitor#_aload_0(int)
 */
public void _aload_0(int pc) {
  dumpPcNumber(pc);
  buffer.append
    (OpcodeStringValues.BYTECODE_NAMES[IOpcodeMnemonics.ALOAD_0]);
  writeNewLine();
}
```

The call to dumpPcNumber can obviously be realized as an aspect. However, in this case aspect-oriented programming can even generate all 205 methods (including comment) since the methods differ only in the name of the bytecode instruction.

3.5.1 Evaluation Setup

For a more thorough evaluation we chose three JAVA open-source projects and mined them for cross-cutting concerns. We refer to Table 3.1 for some statistics.

- JHotDraw 6.0b1 is a GUI framework to build graphical drawing editors. We chose it for its frequent use as aspect mining benchmark.

- Columba 1.0 is an email client that comes with wizards and internationalization support. We chose it because of its well-documented project history.

- ECLIPSE 3.2M3 is an integrated development environment that is based on a plug-in architecture. We chose it because it is a huge project with many developers and a large history.

For each project, we collected the CVS data as described in Section 3.4, mined for simple aspect candidates as defined in Section 3.1, reinforced them using the localities established in Section 3.2, and also built complex aspect candidates as introduced in Section 3.3. We investigated the following questions:

1. *Simple Aspect Candidates.* How precise is our mining approach? That is, how many simple aspect candidates are real cross-cutting concerns?

2. *Reinforcement.* It leads to larger aspect candidates, but does it actually rank true simple aspect candidates high, thus, improving precision?

3. *Ranking.* Can we rank aspect candidates such that more cross-cutting concerns are ranked first?

4. *Complex Aspect Candidates.* How many complex aspect candidates can we find by the combination of simple ones?

To measure *precision*, we computed for each project, ranking, and reinforcement algorithm the top 50 simple aspect candidates. In order to eliminate multiple evaluation effort due to possible duplicates, we combined these rankings into one set per project. For Columba we got 134, for ECLIPSE 159, and for JHotDraw 102 *unique* simple aspect candidates. Next, we sorted these sets alphabetically by the name of the called method in order to prevent bias in the subsequent evaluation. We used this order to

Table 3.1: Summary statistics about the evaluation subjects.

	Columba	ECLIPSE	JHotDraw
Presence			
Lines of code	103,094	1,675,025	57,360
JAVA files	1,633	12,935	974
JAVA methods	4,191	74,612	2,043
History			
Developer	19	137	9
Transactions	4,105	97,900	269
– that changed JAVA files	3,186	77,250	241
– that added method calls	1,820	43,270	132
Method calls added	24,623	430,848	7,517
First transaction	2001-04-08	2001-05-02	2000-10-12
Last transaction	2005-11-02	2005-11-23	2005-04-25

classify simple aspect candidates manually into *true* and *false* cross-cutting concerns. The *precision* is then defined as the ratio of the number of true cross-cutting concerns to the number of aspect candidates that were uncovered by HAM. Precision is basically the accuracy of our technique's results and in general a common measure for search performance.

We considered an aspect candidate (M, L) as a true cross-cutting concern if it referred to the same functionality and the methods M were called in a similar way, i.e., at the same position within a method and with the same parameters. An additional requirement for a true cross-cutting concern was that it can be implemented using AspectJ. However, we did not take into account whether aspect-orientation is the best way to realize the given functionality. In cases of doubt, we classified a candidate as a false cross-cutting concern.

It would also be interesting to measure *recall*: the ratio of correctly identified aspect candidates and all candidates. Recall measures how well a search algorithm finds what is is supposed to find. However, determining recall values requires the knowledge of all aspect candidates—which is impossible for real-world software. We therefore cannot report recall numbers.

3.5.2 Simple Aspect Candidates

To evaluate our notion of simple aspect candidates we checked whether the top-50 candidates per ranking and project were cross-cutting or not. The precision as the ratio of true cross-cutting functionality and all (50) aspect candidates are listed in Table 3.2 for each project (columns) and each ranking (rows).

We observe that precision increases with subject size: It is highest for ECLIPSE and lowest for JHotDraw, the smallest subject. The ranking has a minor impact and no ranking is generally superior; the deviation among the precision values is at most 10 percentage points. Nevertheless, the ranking by size, which simply ranks by the number of locations where a method was added, seems to work well across all projects. It reaches a precision between 36 and 52 percent. Roughly speaking, every second (for JHotDraw every third) mined aspect candidate is a real cross-cutting concern.

Unlike ranking by size, ranking by fragmentation and by compactness take the number of overall modified locations into account. We believe that the poor performance of these rankings for the smaller subjects JHotDraw and Columba is caused by the much smaller number of transactions and added method calls available for mining (hundreds/few thousands versus tens of thousands; see Table 3.1). We expect these results to be better for longer project histories.

3.5.3 Reinforcement

After mining simple aspect candidates we evaluated the effect of reinforcement on them. Reinforcement takes a simple aspect candidate (M, L) from a single transaction and looks at locally related transactions in order to arrive at a candidate (M, L') with an enlarged set $L' \supset L$ of locations. For the evaluation we reinforced the simple aspects using temporal, possessional, and contextual locality, and using all localities applied at once. As before, we checked the top-50 aspect candidates and computed the precision.

Table 3.3 lists the *change in precision* for each subject (columns), each locality (rows), and each ranking by size or compactness (sub-rows). Changes are relative to the precision before reinforcement (Table 3.2). Hence, these changes express the effect of reinforcement on the precision of our mining.[1]

---

[1]Note that for reinforcement we did not rank by fragmentation. This ranking punishes reinforced aspect candidates that are spread across many transactions.

Table 3.2: Precision for simple aspect candidates (in %).

	Columba	ECLIPSE	JHotDraw
Size	52	52	36
Fragmentation	46	54	30
Compactness	42	52	28

Table 3.3: Effect of reinforcement on the precision (in % points).

	Columba	ECLIPSE	JHotDraw
Temporal locality			
Size	+ 2	− 4	± 0
Compactness	+ 2	− 2	+ 4
Possessional locality			
Size	− 8	−20	+ 2
Compactness	+12	+ 8	+ 2
All localities			
Size	− 8	−20	+ 2
Compactness	+10	+ 6	+ 2

Temporal locality produces slight improvements but seems to be unsatisfying for large projects. We presume that this is because we chose the same fixed time window of 2 days for all three subjects; we plan to investigate whether a window size proportional to a project's size would yield better results. The ECLIPSE project has far more developers as well as CVS transactions per day than JHotDraw and Columba. Thus, we have too much noise that diminishes the positive impact of temporal locality for ECLIPSE.

Possessional locality shows the most significant improvement. Albeit ranking by size decreases precision up to 20 percentage points, possessional locality in combination with ranking by compactness improves precision up to 12 percentage points for all three subjects. In large projects, get and set methods are inserted in many locations and thus alleviate the positive effects of possessional locality for ECLIPSE when aspect candidates are ranked by size.

All localities considers the application of both localities. The effect on the precision is the same as with reinforcement based on possessional locality only: ranking by size annihilates the positive impact, ranking by compactness facilitates it. Thus, possessional locality is dominant and affects precision prominently.

The good results for possessional locality suggest that aspects belong to a developer, and are mostly not distributed over many transactions. This is backed up by the notably improved precision of our approach after reinforcement based on possessional locality combined with ranking by compactness. Besides, all our results, without and with reinforcements, suggest that small projects have small histories and thus we achieve a significantly lower precision. In addition, precision can only be improved marginally with reinforcements. This seems consequential as reinforcements leverage a large amount of transactions and developers.

3.5.4 Precision Revisited

So far we have evaluated our mining by computing the precision of the top-50 aspect candidates in a ranking. However, it is unlikely that a developer is really interested in 50 aspect candidates. Instead, she will probably look only at ten or twenty candidates at most. We therefore have broken down the precision for the top ten, twenty, and so on candidates for each project. The results for all three subjects are similar. For the detailed discussion here, we have chosen ECLIPSE for two reasons—it is an industrial-sized project and the results are most meaningful; they are plotted in Figure 3.5.4. The results for Columba and JHotDraw can be found in Figure 3.5.4 and 3.3 respectively.

The graph on the left shows the precision when *ranked by size* before and after applying different reinforcements. The precision stays mostly flat when moving from the top-50 to the top-10 candidates. However, the overall precision remains between 30 and 60 percent. Reinforcement seems to make matters only worse, as ranking by size before reinforcement performs best.

In contrast, the graph on the right shows a dramatically different picture for the precision when *ranked by compactness*. The precision is highest for the top-10 candidates and decreases when additional candidates are taken into account; it is lowest for the top-50 candidates. However, the first ten candidates have a precision of at least 90%. This means, nine out of ten are true cross-cutting concerns. Thus, ranking by compactness is very valuable for developers.

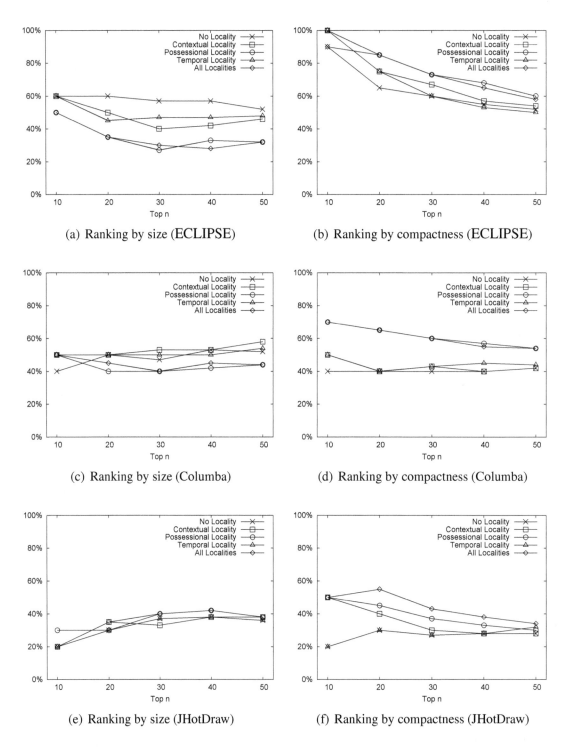

Figure 3.3: Precision of HAM for subjects ECLIPSE, Columba, and JHotDraw.

In summary, size is not the most prominent attribute of cross-cutting concerns, but compactness is. This is also supported by the observation that temporal and possessional locality enhance ranking by compactness.

3.5.5   Complex Aspect Candidates

For our evaluation subjects, we combined simple aspect candidates into a complex candidate if they cross-cut exactly the same locations. This condition was very selective: for Columba we got 21, for ECLIPSE 178, and for JHotDraw 11 complex aspect candidates. Note that all candidates cross-cut at least 8 locations. Below, we discuss the results from ECLIPSE in more detail.

Table 3.4 shows the top 20 complex aspect candidates ranked by size for the ECLIPSE project. Each row represents one complex aspect candidate (M, L). The second column contains the methods M called by an aspect candidate, where the number in brackets denotes the number of arguments for each method. The third column gives the number $|M|$ of methods and the fourth column shows the number $|L|$ of method locations where calls to M were inserted. In the first column we provide the result of our manual inspection of this aspect candidate: ✓ for an actual cross-cutting concern and ✗ for a false positive.

HAM indeed finds cross-cutting concerns consisting of several method calls. In addition, they are ranked on top of the list. However, the performance of our approach decreases when it comes to lower-ranked aspect candidates. We believe that one reason for poor performance are get and set methods that are inserted in many locations at the same time and thus out-rank actual cross-cutting concerns in the number of occurrences. Although these getters and setters are not cross-cutting, they still describe perfect usage patterns.

Furthermore, we find only few complex cross-cutting concerns. This is mainly a consequence of the condition that the locations sets have to be the same ($L_1 = L_2$). We could relax this criterion to the requirement that one location set has to be a subset of the other ($L_1 \subseteq L_2$), however, this adds exponential complexity to the determination of aspect candidates. We will improve on this in our future work. For now, let us look at three cross-cutting concerns in ECLIPSE.

Table 3.4: Complex aspect candidates (M,L) found for ECLIPSE.

	M	$|M|$	$|L|$
✓	$\{\texttt{lock}(0), \texttt{unlock}(0)\}$	2	1284
✓	$\{\texttt{postReplaceChild}(3), \texttt{preReplaceChild}(3)\}$	2	104
✓	$\{\texttt{postLazyInit}(2), \texttt{preLazyInit}(0)\}$	2	78
✗	$\{\texttt{blockSignal}(2), \texttt{unblockSignal}(2)\}$	2	63
✓	$\{\texttt{getLength}(0), \texttt{getStartPosition}(0)\}$	2	62
✓	$\{\texttt{hasChildrenChanges}(1), \texttt{visitChildrenNeeded}(1)\}$	2	62
✗	$\{\texttt{modificationCount}(0), \texttt{setModificationCount}(1)\}$	2	60
✗	$\{\texttt{noMoreAvailableSpaceInConstantPool}(1), \texttt{referenceType}(0)\}$	2	57
✗	$\{\texttt{g\_signal\_handlers\_block\_matched}(7),$		
	$\quad \texttt{g\_signal\_handlers\_unblock\_matched}(7)\}$	2	54
✗	$\{\texttt{getLocalVariableName}(1), \texttt{getLocalVariableName}(2)\}$	2	51
✗	$\{\texttt{isExisting}(1), \texttt{preserve}(1)\}$	2	48
✗	$\{\texttt{isDisposed}(0), \texttt{isTrue}(1)\}$	2	37
✗	$\{\texttt{gtk\_signal\_handler\_block\_by\_data}(2),$		
	$\quad \texttt{gtk\_signal\_handler\_unblock\_by\_data}(2)\}$	2	34
✗	$\{\texttt{error}(1), \texttt{isDisposed}(0)\}$	2	31
✗	$\{\texttt{getWarnings}(0), \texttt{setWarnings}(1)\}$	2	31
✗	$\{\texttt{getCodeGenerationSettings}(1), \texttt{getJavaProject}(0)\}$	2	31
✗	$\{\texttt{SimpleName}(1), \texttt{internalSetIdentifier}(1)\}$	2	29
✗	$\{\texttt{iterator}(0), \texttt{next}(0)\}$	2	27
✓	$\{\texttt{postValueChange}(1), \texttt{preValueChange}(1)\}$	2	26
✗	$\{\texttt{SimpleName}(1), \texttt{internalSetIdentifier}(1)\}$	2	25

Locking Mechanism. This cross-cutting concern was already mentioned in the introduction to this chapter. Calls to both methods lock and unlock were inserted in 1,284 method locations. Here is such a location:

```
public static final native void _XFree(int address);
public static final void XFree(int /*long*/ address) {
    lock.lock();
    try {
        _XFree(address);
    } finally {
        lock.unlock();
    }
}
```

The other 1,283 method locations look similar. First lock is called, then a corresponding native method, and finally unlock. It is a typical example of a cross-cutting concern which can be easily realized using AOP. Note that this lock/unlock concern cross-cuts different platforms. It appears in both the GTK and Motif version of ECLIPSE. Typically such cross-platform concerns are recognized incompletely by static and dynamic aspect mining approaches unless the platforms are analyzed separately and results combined.

Abstract Syntax Trees.   ECLIPSE represents nodes of abstract syntax trees (ASTs) by the abstract class ASTNode and several subclasses. These subclasses fall into the following simplified *categories*: expressions (Expression), statements (Statement), and types (Type). Additionally, each subclass of ASTNode has *properties* that cross-cut the class hierarchy. An example for a property is the *name* of a node: There are named (QualifiedType) and unnamed types (PrimitiveType), as well as named expressions (FieldAccess). Additional properties of a node include the *type*, *expression*, *operator*, or *body*.

This is a typical example of a *role super-imposition* concern (Marin et al., 2005). As a result, every named subclass of ASTNode implements method setName which results in duplicated code. With AOP the concern could be realised via the method-introduction mechanism.

```
public void setName(SimpleName name) {
   if (name == null) {
      throw new IllegalArgumentException();
   }
   ASTNode oldChild = this.methodName;
   preReplaceChild(oldChild, name, NAME_PROPERTY);
   this.methodName = name;
   postReplaceChild(oldChild, name, NAME_PROPERTY);
}
```

Our mining approach revealed this cross-cutting concern with several aspect candidates. The methods preReplaceChild and postReplaceChild are called in the setName method; the methods preLazyInit and postLazyInit guarantee the safe initialization of properties; and the methods preValueChange and postValueChange are called when a new operator is set for a node.

Cloning.   Another cross-cutting concern was surprising because it involved two getter methods getStartPosition and getLength. These are always called in clone0
of subclasses of ASTNode and were also identified by our approach.

```
ASTNode clone0(AST target) {
   BooleanLiteral result = new BooleanLiteral(target);
   result.setSourceRange(this.getStartPosition(),
                       this.getLength());
   result.setBooleanValue(booleanValue());
   return result;
}
```

3.6   Related Work

Related work falls into two categories: aspect mining and mining software repositories.

3.6.1   Aspect Mining

Previous approaches to aspect mining considered a program only at a particular time,
using traditional static and dynamic program analysis techniques. One fundamental
problem is their scalability. While dynamic analysis strongly depends on a compil-
able, executable program version and on the coverage of the used program test cases,
static analyses often produce too many details and false positives as they cannot weed
out non-executable code. To overcome these limitations, each approach would need
additional methods which in turn make them then far less practical. Besides, many
approaches require user interaction or even previous knowledge about the program.

Griswold et al. (1999) present the Aspect Browser which identifies cross-cutting concerns with textual-pattern matching (much like "grep") and highlights them. The Aspect Mining Tool (AMT) by Hannemann and Kiczales (2001) combines text- and type-
based analysis of source code. Ophir uses a control-based comparison, applying code
clone detection on program dependence graphs (Shepherd and Pollock, 2003). Tourwé
and Mens (2004) introduce an identifier analysis based on formal concept analysis for
mining aspectual views such as structurally related classes and methods. Krinke and
Breu (2004) propose an automatic static aspect mining based on control flow. The control flow graph of a program is mined for recurring execution patterns of methods. The

fan-in analysis by Marin et al. (2004, 2007) determines methods that are called from many different places—thus having a high fan-in. Our approach is similar since we analyse how fan-in changed over time. In future work, we will investigate how this additional information increases precision.

The Dynamic Aspect Mining Tool (DynAMiT) by (Breu, 2004; Breu and Krinke, 2004) analyzes program traces reflecting the run-time behavior of a system in search for re-curring execution patterns of method relations. Tonella and Ceccato (2004) suggest a technique that applies concept analysis to the relationship between execution traces and executed computational units.

Loughran and Rashid (2002) investigate possible representations of aspects found in a legacy system in order to provide best tool support for aspect mining. Breu (2005) also reports on a hybrid approach where the dynamic information of the previous DynAMiT approach is complemented with static type information such as static object types.

3.6.2   Mining Software Repositories

One of the most frequently used techniques for mining version archives is co-change. The basic idea is simple: *Two items that are changed together in the same transaction, are related to each other.* Our approach is also based on co-change. However, we use a different, more specific notion of co-change. Methods are part of a (simple) aspect candidate when they are changed together in the same transaction and *additionally the changes are the same*, i.e., a call to the same method is inserted.

Recently, research extended the idea of co-change to *additions* and applied this concept to method calls: *Two method calls that are inserted together in the same transaction, are related to each other.* Williams and Hollingsworth (2005a) use this observation to mine pairs of functions that form usage patterns from version archives. In Chapter 2, we used data mining to locate patterns of arbitrary size and applied dynamic analysis to validate their patterns and identify violations. The work in this chapter also investigates the addition of method calls. However, HAM does not focus on calls that are inserted together, but on *locations where the same call is inserted*. This allows us to identify cross-cutting concerns rather than usage patterns.

3.7 Summary

This chapter introduced the first approach to use version history to mine aspect candidates. The underlying hypothesis is that cross-cutting concerns emerge over time. By introducing the dimension of time, our aspect mining approach has the following advantages:

1. HAM *scales to industrial-sized projects* like ECLIPSE. In particular, HAM reaches higher precision (above 90%) for big projects with a long history. Additionally, HAM focuses on concerns that cross-cut huge parts of a system. For small projects, HAM suffers from the much fewer data available, resulting in lower precision (about 60%).

2. HAM *discovers cross-cutting concerns across platform-specific code* (see `lock/unlock` in Section 3.5.5). Static and dynamic approaches recognize such concerns only when the code base is mined multiple times.

3. HAM *yields a high precision*. The average precision is around 50%, however, precision increases up to 90% with the project size and history.

Part II

Predicting Defects

4

Defects and Dependencies

Software errors cost the U.S. industry 60 billion dollars a year according to a study conducted by the National Institute of Standards and Technology (Tassey, 2002). One contributing factor to the high number of errors is the limitation of resources for quality assurance (QA). Such resources are always limited by *time*, e.g., the deadlines that development teams face, and by *cost*, e.g., not enough people are available for QA. When managers want to spend resources most effectively, they would typically allocate them on the parts where they expect most defects or at least the most severe ones. Put in other words: *based on their experience, managers predict the quality* of the product to make further decisions on testing, inspections, etc.

In order to support managers with this task, research identified several quality indicators and developed prediction models to predict the quality of software parts. The complexity of source code is one of the most prominent indicators for such models. However, even though several studies showed McCabe's cyclomatic complexity to correlate with the number of defects (Basili et al., 1996; Nagappan et al., 2006b; Subramanyam and Krishnan, 2003), there is no universal metric or prediction model that applies to all projects (Nagappan et al., 2006b). One drawback of most complexity metrics is that they only focus on single elements, but rarely take the interactions between elements into account. However, with the advent of static and dynamic bug localization techniques, the nature of defects has changed and today most defects in bug databases are of semantic nature (Li et al., 2006).

In this part we will pay special attention to interactions between elements. More precisely, we will investigate how dependencies correlate with and predict defects in Windows Server 2003. While this is not the first work on defects and dependencies, we will cover a different angle: In order to identify the binaries that are most central in Windows Server 2003, we apply *network analysis* on dependency graphs. Network analysis is very popular in social sciences where networks between humans (actors) and their interactions (ties) are studied. In our context the binaries are the "actors" and the dependencies are the "ties" (Chapter 5). We will also apply complexity measures from graph theory to identify the subsystems of Windows Server 2003 that are most defect-prone (Chapter 6).

Before we discuss related work, we will briefly motivate the use of dependencies for defect prediction with several observations that we made for Windows Server 2003.

4.1 Motivation

When we analyzed defect data and dependency graphs for Windows Server 2003, we made the following observations.

Cycles had on average twice as many defects.

We investigated whether the presence of dependency cycles has an impact on defects. A simple example for a dependency cycle is a mutual dependency, i.e., binaries X and Y depend on each other; for this experiment, we considered cycles of any size, but ignored self-cycles such as X depends on X. Based on whether binaries are part of a cycle, we divided them into groups. Binaries that were part of *cycles had on average twice as many defects* as the other binaries, at a significance level of 99%.

Central binaries tend to be defect-prone.

We identified several network motifs in the dependency graph of Windows Server 2003. Network motifs are patterns that describe similar, but not necessarily isomorphic sub-

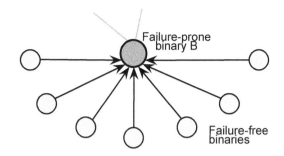

Figure 4.1: Star pattern in dependency graphs.

graphs; originally they were introduced in biological research (Milo et al., 2002). One of the motifs for Windows Server 2003 looks like a star (see Figure 4.1): it consists of a binary B that is connected to the main component of the dependency graph. Several other "satellite" binaries surround B and exclusively depend on binary B. In most occurrences of the pattern, the binary B was defect-prone, while the satellite binaries were defect-free. Social network analysis identifies binary B as *central* (a so-called 'Broker") in the dependency graph because it controls its satellite binaries.

We conjecture that binaries that are identified as central by network analysis are more defect-prone than others (Chapter 5).

The larger a clique, the more defect-prone are its binaries.

A clique is a set of binaries for which between every pair of binaries (X, Y) a dependency exists—we neglect the direction, i.e., it does not matter whether X depends on Y, Y on X, or both. Figure 4.2 shows an example for an undirected clique; a clique is maximal if no other binary can be added without losing the clique property. We enumerated all *maximal undirected cliques* in the dependency graph of Windows Server 2003 with the Bron-Kerbosch algorithm (Bron and Kerbosch, 1973). The enumeration of cliques is a core component in many biological applications. Next we grouped the cliques by size and computed the *average number of defects* per binary.

Figure 4.3 shows the results, including a 95% confidence interval of the average. We can observe that the *average number of defects increases with the size of the clique a binary resides in.* Put in another way, binaries that are part of more complex areas (cliques) have more defects.

Again, this observation motivates network analysis: binaries that are part of cliques

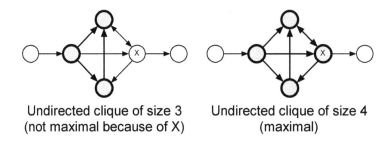

Undirected clique of size 3   Undirected clique of size 4
(not maximal because of X)   (maximal)

Figure 4.2: An example for undirected cliques.

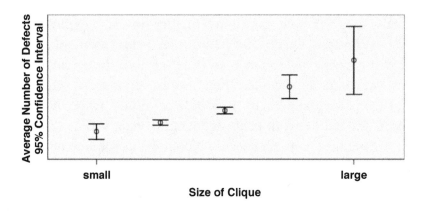

Figure 4.3: Average number of defects for binaries in small vs. large cliques.

are close to each other, which is measured by the network measure *closeness*. We hypothesize that closeness, as well as other network measures, correlates with the number of defects (Chapter 5). It also motivates complexity measures on subgraphs: *the more dense the dependencies of a subsystem, the more defects it is likely to have* (Chapter 6).

4.2   Related Work

In this section we discuss related work; it falls into four categories: social network analysis in software engineering, software dependencies, complexity metrics, and analysis of historical data.

4.2.1   Social Network Analysis in Software Engineering

The use of social network analysis is not new to software engineering. Several researchers used social network analysis to study the dynamics of open source development. Ghosh showed that many SourceForge.net projects are organized as self-organizing social networks (Ghosh, 2003). Madey et al. (2002) conducted a similar study where they focused on collaboration aspects by looking at the joint-membership of developers in projects. In addition to committer networks, Lopez-Fernandez et al. (2004) investigated module networks that show how several modules relate to each other. Ohira et al. (2005) used social networks and collaborative filtering to support the identification of experts across projects. Huang and Liu (2005) used historical data to identify core and peripheral development teams in software projects.

Social network analysis was also used on research networks. Hassan and Holt (2004) analyzed the reverse engineering community using co-authorship relations. They also identified emerging research trends and directions over time and compared reverse engineering to the entire software engineering community.

In contrast to these approaches, we do not analyze the relations between developers or projects, but rather between binaries of a single project. Also the objective of our study is different. While most of the existing work considered organizational aspects, our aim is to predict defects.

4.2.2   Software Dependencies

Pogdurski and Clarke (1990) presented a formal model of program dependencies as the relationship between two pieces of code inferred from the program text. Program dependencies have also been analyzed in terms of testing (Korel, 1987), code optimization and parallelization (Ferrante et al., 1987), and debugging (Orso et al., 2004). Empirical studies have also investigated dependencies and program predicates (Binkley and Harman, 2003) and inter-procedural control dependencies (Sinha et al., 2001) in programming language research.

The information-flow metric defined by Henry and Kafura. (1981), uses *fan-in* (a count of the number of modules that call a given module) and *fan-out* (a count of the number of modules that are called by a given module) to calculate a complexity metric. Components with a large fan-in and large fan-out may indicate poor design. In contrast, our work uses not only calls, but also data dependencies. Furthermore, we distinguish between different types such as intra-dependencies and outgoing dependencies.

Schröter et al. (2006) showed that the actual import dependencies (not just the count) can predict defects, e.g., importing compiler packages is riskier than importing UI packages. Earlier work on dependencies at Microsoft (Nagappan and Ball, 2007) showed that code churn and dependencies can be used as efficient indicators of post-release defects. The basic idea being, for example suppose that component A has many dependencies on component B. If the code of component B changes (churns) a lot between versions, we may expect that component A will need to undergo a certain amount of churn in order to keep in sync with component B. That is, churn often will propagate across dependencies. Together, a high degree of dependence plus churn can cause errors that will propagate through a system, reducing its reliability.

4.2.3 Historical Data

Several researchers used historical data for predicting defect density: Khoshgoftaar et al. (1996) classified modules as defect-prone when the number of lines added or deleted exceeded a given threshold. Graves et al. (2000) used the sum of contributions to a module to predict defect density. Ostrand et al. (2005) used historical data from up to 17 releases to predict the files with the highest defect density of the next release. Further, Mockus et al. (2005) predicted the customer perceived quality using logistic regression for a commercial telecommunications system (of size seven million lines of code) by utilizing external factors like hardware configurations, software platforms, amount of usage and deployment issues. They observed an increase in probability of failure by twenty times by accounting for such measures in their prediction equations.

4.2.4 Complexity Metrics

Typically, research on defect-proneness captures software complexity with metrics and builds models that relate these metrics to defect-proneness (Denaro et al., 2002). Basili et al. (1996) were among the first to validate that OO metrics predict defect density. Subramanyam and Krishnan (2003) presented a survey on eight more empirical studies, all showing that OO metrics are significantly associated with defects. Briand et al. (1997) identified several coupling measures that could serve as early quality indicators.

Our experiments focus on post-release defects since they matter most for the end-users of a program. Only few studies addressed post-release defects: Binkley and Schach (1998) developed a coupling metric and showed that it outperforms several other metrics; Ohlsson and Alberg (1996) used metrics to predict modules that fail during operation. Additionally, within five Microsoft projects, Nagappan et al. (2006b) identified metrics that predict post-release defects and reported how to systematically build predictors for post-release defects from history. In contrast to their work, we develop new metrics on dependency data from a graph theoretic point of view.

5

Predicting Defects for Binaries

In this chapter we will compute measures from network analysis on dependency graphs. More formally, the hypotheses that we will investigate are the following:

H1 *Network measures on dependency graphs can indicate critical binaries that are missed by complexity metrics.*

H2 *Network measures on dependency graphs correlate positively with the number of post-release defects*—an increase in a measure is accompanied by an increase in defects.

H3 *Network measures on dependency graphs, can predict the number of post-release defects.*

H4 *Depending on certain binaries increases the likelihood of a failure of a binary* (domino effect).

The outline of this chapter is as follows. First, we will present the data collection for our study: for Windows Server 2003 we computed dependencies, complexity metrics, and measures from network analysis (Section 5.1). In our experiments, we evaluated

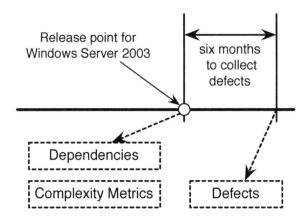

Figure 5.1: Data collection in Windows Server 2003.

network measures against complexity metrics. Additionally, we show that network analysis succeeds in identifying binaries that are considered as most harmful by developers and present empirical evidence for the domino effect (Section 5.2). We close with a discussion of threats to validity (Section 5.3).

5.1 Data Collection

For our experiments we build a dependency graph of Windows Server 2003 (Section 5.1.1) and compute network measures on it (Section 5.1.2). Additionally, we collect complexity metrics (Section 5.1.3) which we use to quantify the contribution of network analysis. The data collection is illustrated in Figure 5.1.

5.1.1 Dependency Graph

A software dependency is a directed relation between two pieces of code (such as expressions or methods). There exist different kinds of dependencies: *data dependencies* between the definition and use of values and *call dependencies* between the declaration of functions and the sites where they are called. Microsoft has an automated tool called MaX (Srivastava et al., 2005) that tracks dependency information at the function level, including calls, imports, exports, RPC, COM, and Registry access. MaX generates a system-wide dependency graph from both native x86 and .NET managed binaries.

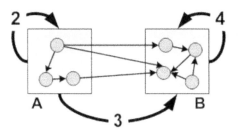

Figure 5.2: Lifting up dependencies to binary level. The edges are labeled by the multiplicity of a dependency.

Within Microsoft, MaX is used for change impact analysis and for integration testing (Srivastava et al., 2005).

For our analysis, we use MaX to generate a system-wide dependency graph at the function level. Since we collect defect data for binaries, we lift this graph up to binary level in a separate post-processing step. Consider for example the dependency graph in Figure 5.2. Circles denote functions and boxes are binaries. Each thin edge corresponds to a dependency at function level. Lifting them up to binary level, there are two dependencies within A and four within B (represented by self-edges), as well as three dependencies where A depends on B. We refer to these numbers as *multiplicity* of a dependency/edge.

As a result of this lifting operation there may be several dependencies between a pair of binaries (like in Figure 5.2 between A and B), which results in several edges in the dependency graph. Formally a dependency graph is a therefore directed multigraph $G_M = (V, A)$ where

- V is a set of nodes (binaries) and

- $A = (E, m)$ a multiset of edges (dependencies) for which $E \subseteq V \times V$ contains the actual edges and the function $m : E \rightarrow N$ returns the multiplicity (count) of an edge.

The corresponding regular graph (without multiedges) is $G = (V, E)$. We allow self-edges (i.e., a binary can depend on itself) for both regular graphs and multigraphs.

For the experiments in this chapter, we use only the regular graph G. When predicting defects for subsystems, we will take multiplicities into account (Chapter 6).

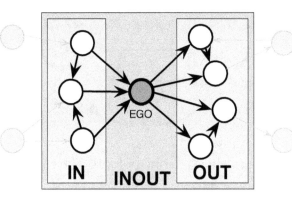

Figure 5.3: Different neighborhoods in an ego-network.

5.1.2   Network Measures

On the dependency graph we computed for each node (binary) a number of network measures by using the Ucinet 6 tool (Borgatti et al., 2002). In this section, we will describe these measures more in detail, however, for or a more comprehensive overview, we refer to textbooks on social network analysis (Hanneman and Riddle, 2005; Wasserman and Faust, 1984).

5.1.2.1   Ego Networks vs. Global Networks

One important distinction made in social network analysis is between *ego networks* and *global networks*.

Every node in a network has a corresponding ego network that describes how the node is connected to its neighbors. (Nodes are often referred to as "ego" in network analysis.) Figure 5.3 explains how ego networks are constructed. In our case, they contain the ego binary itself, binaries that depend on the ego (IN), binaries on which the ego depends (OUT), and the dependencies between these binaries. The ego network would thus be the subgraph within the INOUT box of Figure 5.3.

In contrast, the global network corresponds always to the entire dependency graph. While ego networks allow us to measure the local importance of a binary with respect to its neighbors, global networks reveal the importance of a binary within the entire software system. Since we expected local and global importance to complement each other, we used both in our study.

Table 5.1: Network measures for ego networks.

Measure	Description
Size	The size of the ego network is the number of nodes.
Ties	The number of directed ties corresponds to the number of edges.
Pairs	The number of ordered pairs is the maximal number of directed ties, i.e., $Size \times (Size-1)$.
Density	The percentage of possible ties that are actually present, i.e., $Ties/Pairs$.
WeakComp	The number of weak components (=sets of connected binaries) in neighborhood.
nWeakComp	The number of weak components normalized by size, i.e., $WeakComp/Size$.
TwoStepReach	The percentage of nodes that are two steps away.
ReachEfficency	The reach efficiency normalizes TwoStepReach by size, i.e., $TwoStepReach/Size$. High reach efficiency indicates that ego's primary contacts are influential in the network.
Brokerage	The number of pairs not directly connected. The higher this number, the more paths go through ego, i.e., ego acts as a "broker" in its network.
nBrokerage	The Brokerage normalized by the number of pairs, i.e., $Brokerage/Pairs$.
EgoBetween	The percentage of *shortest* paths between neighbors that pass through ego.
nEgoBetween	The Betweenness normalized by the size of the ego network.

5.1.2.2 Ego Networks

An ego network for a binary consists of its neighborhood in the dependency graph. We distinguish between three kinds of neighborhoods (see also Figure 5.3):

- *In-neighborhood (IN)* contains the binaries that depend on the ego binary.

- *Out-neighborhood (OUT)* contains the binaries on which the ego binary depends.

- *InOut-neighborhood (INOUT)* combines the In- and Out-neighborhoods.

For every binary, we induce its three ego networks (one for each kind of neighborhood) and compute fairly basic measures that are listed in Table 5.1. Additionally, we compute measures for structural holes that are described below.

5.1.2.3 Global Network

Within the global network (=dependency graph) we can measure the importance of binaries for the whole software system and not only their local neighborhood. For most network measures we use directed edges; however, some measures can be applied to symmetric, undirected networks *(Sym)* or ingoing *(In)* and outgoing *(Out)* edges respectively. On the global network, we compute measures for structural holes and centrality. Both concepts are summarized below.

5.1.2.4 Structural Holes

The term of structural holes was coined by Burt (1995). Ideally, the influence of actors is balanced in social networks. The Figure below shows two networks for three actors A, B, and C.

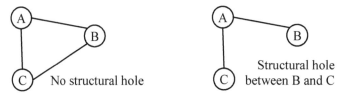

In the left network all actors are tied to each other and therefore have the same influence. In the network on the right hand side, the tie between B and C is missing ("structural hole"), giving A an advanced position over B and C.

We used the following measures related to structural holes in our study of dependency graphs:

- *Effective size of network (EffSize)* is the number of binaries that are connected to a binary X minus the average number of ties between these binaries. Suppose X has three neighbors that are not connected to each other, then the effective size of X's ego network is 3–0=3. If each of the three neighbors would be connected to the other ones, the average number of ties would be two, and the effective size of X's ego network reduces to 3–2=1.

- *Efficiency* norms the effective size of a network to the total size of the network.

- *Constraint* measures how strongly a binary is constrained by its neighbors. The idea is that neighbors that are connected to other neighbors can constrain a binary. For more details we refer to Burt (1995).

- *Hierarchy* measures how the constraint measure is distributed across neighbors. When most of the constraint comes from a single neighbor, the value for hierarchy is higher. For more details we refer to Burt (1995).

The values for the above measures are higher for binaries with neighbors that are closely connected to each other and other binaries. One might expect that such complex dependency structures result in a higher number of defects.

5.1.2.5 Centrality Measures

One of the most frequently used concepts in social network analysis (Hanneman and Riddle, 2005; Wasserman and Faust, 1984) is *centrality*. It is used to identify actors that are in "favored positions". Applied on dependency graphs, centrality identifies the binaries that are specially exposed to dependencies, e.g., by being the target of many dependents. There are different approaches to measure centrality:

- *Degree centrality*. The degree measures the number of dependencies for a binary. The idea for dependency graphs is that binaries with many dependencies are more defect-prone than others.

- *Closeness centrality*. While degree centrality measures only the immediate dependencies of a binary, closeness centrality additionally takes the distance to all other binaries into account. There are different variants to compute closeness:

    - *Closeness* is the sum of the lengths of the shortest (geodesic) paths from a binary (or to a binary) from all other binaries. There exist different variations of closeness in social network analysis. Our definition corresponds to the one used by Freeman (see (Hanneman and Riddle, 2005; Wasserman and Faust, 1984)).
    - *dwReach* is the number of binaries that can be reached from a binary (or which can reach a binary). The distance is weighted by the number of steps with factors 1/1, 1/2, 1/3, etc.
    - *Eigenvector centrality* is similar to Google's PageRank value (Cho et al., 1998); it assigns relative scores to all binaries in the dependency graphs. Dependencies to binaries having a high score contribute more to the score of the binary in question.
    - *Information centrality* is the harmonic mean of the length of paths ending at a binary. The value is smaller for binaries that are connected to other binaries through many short paths.

    Again, the hypothesis is that a more central binary, will have more defects.

- *Betweenness centrality* measures for a binary on how many shortest paths between other binaries it occurs. The hypothesis is that binaries that are part of many shortest paths are more likely to contain defects because defects propagate.

Table 5.2: Metrics used in the Windows Server 2003 study.

Metric	Description
Module metrics for a binary B:	
Function	# functions in B
GlobalVariables	# global variables in B
Per-function metrics for a function f():	
Lines	# executable lines in f()
Parameters	# parameters in f()
FanIn	# functions calling f()
FanOut	# functions called by f()
Complexity	McCabe's cyclomatic complexity of f()
OO metrics for a class C	
ClassMethods	# methods in C
SubClasses	# subclasses of C
InheritanceDepth	Depth of C in the inheritance tree
ClassCoupling	Coupling between classes
CyclicClassCoupling	Cyclic coupling between classes

5.1.3 Complexity Metrics

In order to quantify the contribution of network analysis on dependency graphs, we use code metrics as a control set for providing a comparison point. For each binary, we computed several code metrics, described in Table 5.2. These metrics apply to a binary B and to a function or method $f()$, respectively. In order to have all metrics apply to binaries, we summarized the function metrics across each binary. For each function metric X, we computed the *total* and the *maximum* value per binary (denoted as *TotalX* and *MaxX*, respectively). As an example, consider the *Lines* metric, counting the number of executable lines per function. The *MaxLines* metric indicates the length of the largest function in a binary, while *TotalLines*, the sum of all *Lines*, represents the total number of executable lines in a binary.

5.2 Experimental Analysis

In this section, we will support our hypotheses that network analysis of dependency graphs helps to predict the number of defects for binaries.

We carried out several experiments for Windows Server 2003: First we show that network analysis can identify critical "escrow" binaries (Section 5.2.1). We continue with a correlation analysis of network measures, metrics, and number of defects (Section 5.2.2) and regression models for defect prediction (Section 5.2.3). Finally, we present evidence for a domino effect in Windows Server 2003: binaries that depend on defect-prone binaries are more likely to have defects (Section 5.2.4).

5.2.1 Escrow Analysis

The development teams of Windows Server 2003 maintain a list of critical binaries that are called *escrow binaries*. Whenever programmers change an escrow binary, they must adhere to a special protocol to ensure the stability of Windows Server. Among others, this protocol involves more extensive testing and code reviews on the binary and its related dependencies. In other words these escrow binaries are the "most important" binaries in Windows. An example escrow binary would be the Windows kernel binary. The developers manually select the binaries in the escrow based on past experience with previous builds, changes, and defects.

We used the network measures and complexity metrics (from Sections 5.1.2 and 5.1.3) to predict the list of escrow binaries. For each measure/metric, we ranked the binaries according to its value and took the top N binaries as the prediction, with N being the size of the escrow list. In order to evaluate the predictions, we computed the recall that is the percentage of escrow binaries that we successfully could retrieve. In order to protect proprietary information, i.e., the size of the escrow list, we report only percentages that are truncated to the next multiple of 5%. For instance, the percentage of 23% would be reported as 20%.

The results in Table 5.3 show that complexity metrics fail to predict escrow binaries. They can retrieve only 30%, while the network measures for closeness centrality *can retrieve twice as much.* This observation supports our first hypothesis that *network measures on dependency graphs can indicate critical binaries that are missed by complexity metrics (H1).* Being complex does not make a binary critical in software development—it is more likely the combination of being complex and central to the system.

Table 5.3: Recall for Escrow binaries.

Network measures	Recall
GlobalInClosenessFreeman	0.60
GlobalIndwReach	0.60
EgoInSize	0.55
EgoInPairs	0.55
EgoInBroker	0.55
EgoInTies	0.50
GlobalInDegree	0.50
GlobalBetweenness	0.50
...	...
Complexity metric	**Recall**
TotalParameters	0.30
TotalComplexity	0.30
TotalLines	0.30
TotalFanIn	0.30
TotalFanOut	0.30
...	....

5.2.2 Correlation Analysis

In order to investigate our hypothesis H2, we determined the Pearson and Spearman correlation between the number of defects and each network measure (Section 5.1.2) as well as each complexity metric (Section 5.1.3). The Pearson bivariate correlation requires data to be distributed normally and the association between elements to be linear. In contrast, the Spearman rank correlation is a robust technique that can be applied even when the association between values is non-linear (Fenton and Pfleeger, 1998). For completeness we compute both correlations coefficients. The closer the value of correlation is to −1 or +1, the higher two measures are correlated—positively for +1 and negatively for −1. A value of 0 indicates that two measures are independent.

The Spearman correlation values for Windows Server 2003 are shown in Table 5.2.2. The table consists of three parts: ego network measures, global network measures, and complexity metrics. The columns distinguish between different neighborhoods (IN, OUT, INOUT) and directions of edges (ingoing, outgoing, symmetric). Correlations that are significant at 0.99 are indicated with (*). The values for Pearson correlation are listed in the similarly structured Table 5.2.2.

We can make the following observations.

1. *Some network measures do not correlate with the number of defects.* The correlations for the number of weak components in a neighborhood (WeakComp), the Hierarchy and the Efficiency are all close to zero, which means that their values and the number of defects are independent.

2. *Some network measures have negative correlation coefficients.* The normalized number of weak components in a neighborhood (nWeakComp) as well as the Reach Efficiency and the Constraint show a negative correlation between -0.424 and -0.463. This means that an increase in centrality comes with a decrease in number of defects. Since the values for the aforementioned measures are higher for binaries with neighbors that are closely connected to each other and other binaries, this suggests that being in a closely connected neighborhood does not necessarily result in a high number of defects. This explanation is also supported by the negative correlation of -0.320 for Density.

3. *Network measures have higher correlations for OUT and INOUT than for IN neighborhoods.* In other words, outgoing dependencies are more related to defects than ingoing dependencies. Schröter et al. (2006) found similar evidence and used the targets of outgoing dependencies to predict defects. The measures with the highest observed correlations were related to the *size of the neighborhoods* (Size, Pairs, Broker, EffSize, and Degree) and to *centrality* (Eigenvector and Information), all of them had correlations of 0.400 or higher.

4. *Most complexity metrics have slightly higher correlations than network measures.* For non-OO metrics the correlations are above 0.500. In contrast, for OO metrics the correlations are lower (around 0.300) because not all parts of Windows Server 2003 are developed with object-oriented programming languages. This shows that OO metrics are only of limited use for predicting defects in heterogeneous systems.

To summarize, we could observe significant correlations for most network measures, and most of them were positive and moderate. However, since we observed several negative correlations, we need to remove the "positively" from our initial hypothesis (H2). The revised hypothesis that *network measures on dependency graphs correlate with the number of post-release defects (H2*)* is confirmed by our observations. At a first glance complexity metrics might outperform network measures, but we show in Section 5.2.3 that network measures actually improve prediction models for defects.

Ego Network	Spearman Correlation		
	In	Out	InOut
Size	.283(**)	.440(**)	.462(**)
Ties	.245(**)	.434(**)	.455(**)
Pairs	.276(**)	.440(**)	.462(**)
Density	.253(**)	-.273(**)	-.320(**)
WeakComp	.274(**)	.035	.082(**)
nWeakComp	.227(**)	-.438(**)	-.453(**)
TwoStepReach	.287(**)	.326(**)	.333(**)
ReachEfficency	.230(**)	-.402(**)	-.424(**)
Brokerage	.271(**)	.438(**)	.461(**)
nBrokerage	.283(**)	.275(**)	.321(**)
EgoBetween	.263(**)	.292(**)	.320(**)
nEgoBetween	.279(**)	.294(**)	.285(**)
EffSize			.466(**)
Efficiency			.262(**)
Constraint			-.463(**)
Hierarchy			.064(**)

Global Network			
Eigenvector			.428(**)
Fragmentation			.276(**)
Betweenness			.319(**)
Information			.446(**)
Power			.397(**)
EffSize			.455(**)
Efficiency			.021
Constraint			-.454(**)
Hierarchy			.176(**)

	Ingoing	Outgoing	Symmetric
Closeness	-.057(**)	.284(**)	.372(**)
Degree	.283(**)	.440(**)	.462(**)
dwReach	.285(**)	.394(**)	.379(**)

Complexity Metrics	Max	Total
Functions		.507(**)
GlobalVariables		.436(**)
Lines	.317(**)	.516(**)
Parameters	.386(**)	.521(**)
FanIn	.452(**)	.502(**)
FanOut	.360(**)	.493(**)
Complexity	.310(**)	.509(**)

OO Metrics	Max	Total
ClassMethods	.315(**)	.336(**)
SubClasses	.296(**)	.295(**)
InheritanceDepth	.286(**)	.308(**)
ClassCoupling	.318(**)	.327(**)
CyclicClassCoupling		.331(**)

Table 5.4: Spearman correlation values between the number of defects and network measures as well as complexity metrics.

Correlations significant at 99% are marked by (**). Correlations above 0.40 are printed boldface.

	Pearson Correlation		
Ego Network	**In**	**Out**	**InOut**
Size	.208(**)	**.419(**)**	.234(**)
Ties	.190(**)	**.421(**)**	.242(**)
Pairs	.152(**)	**.424(**)**	.154(**)
Density	.110(**)	-.266(**)	-.336(**)
WeakComp	.187(**)	.051(*)	.178(**)
nWeakComp	.130(**)	-.201(**)	-.215(**)
TwoStepReach	.288(**)	.041	.051(*)
ReachEfficency	.155(**)	-.200(**)	-.226(**)
Brokerage	.152(**)	**.413(**)**	.153(**)
nBrokerge	.270(**)	.269(**)	.338(**)
EgoBetween	.156(**)	.265(**)	.164(**)
nEgoBetween	.198(**)	.329(**)	.290(**)
EffSize			.221(**)
Efficiency			.308(**)
Constraint			-.346(**)
Hierarchy			.208(**)
Global Network			
Eigenvector			.311(**)
Fragmentation			.261(**)
Betweenness			.265(**)
Information			.286(**)
Power			.367(**)
EffSize			.223(**)
Efficiency			.070(**)
Constraint			-.232(**)
Hierarchy			-.041

	Ingoing	**Outgoing**	**Symmetric**
Closeness	.005	.285(**)	.133(**)
Degree	.208(**)	**.419(**)**	.234(**)
dwReach	.302(**)	.252(**)	.133(**)

Complexity metrics	**Max**	**Total**
Functions		**.416(**)**
GlobalVariables		**.466(**)**
Lines	.243(**)	**.557(**)**
Parameters	.391(**)	**.533(**)**
FanIn	.345(**)	**.461(**)**
FanOut	.166(**)	**.480(**)**
Complexity	.049(*)	**.523(**)**

OO metrics	**Max**	**Total**
ClassMethods	.231(**)	.288(**)
SubClasses	.157(**)	.189(**)
InheritanceDepth	.218(**)	.185(**)
ClassCoupling	.224(**)	.210(**)
CyclicClassCoupling		.223(**)

Table 5.5: Pearson correlation values between the number of defects and centrality measures as well as complexity metrics.

Correlations significant at 99% are marked by (**); correlations significant at 95% are marked by (*). Correlations above 0.40 are printed bold.

5.2.3   Regression Analysis

Since network measures on dependency graphs correlate with post-release defects, can we use them to predict defects? To answer this question, we build multiple linear regression (MLR) models where the number of post-release defects forms the dependent variable. We build separate models for three different sets of input variables:

SNA. This set of variables consists of the network measures that were introduced in Section 5.1.2.

METRICS. This set consists of all non-OO complexity metrics listed in Table 5.2. We decided to ignore OO-metrics for the regression analysis because they were only applicable to a part of Windows Server 2003 because most of Windows is comprised of non-OO code.

SNA+METRICS. This set is the combination of the two previous sets (SNA, MET-RICS) and allows us to quantify the value added by network measures.

We carried out six experiments: one for each combination out of two kinds of regression models (linear, logistic) and three sets of input variables (SNA, METRICS, SNA+METRICS).

5.2.3.1   Principal Component Analysis

One difficulty associated with MLR is *multicollinearity* among the independent variables. Multicollinearity comes from inter-correlations amongst metrics such as between the aforementioned *Multi_Edges* and *Multi_Complexity*. Inter-correlations can lead to an inflated variance in the estimation of the dependent variable. To overcome this problem, we use a standard statistical approach called *Principal Component Analysis* (PCA) (Jackson, 2003).

With PCA, a small number of uncorrelated linear combinations of variables are selected for use in regression (linear or logistic). These combinations are independent and thus do not suffer from multicollinearity, while at the same time they account for as much sample variance as possible—for our experiments we selected principal components that account for a cumulative sample variance greater than 95%.

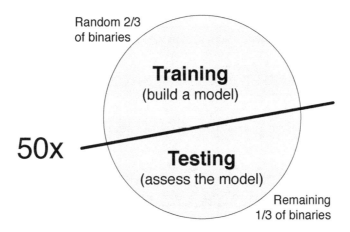

Figure 5.4: Random split experiments.

We ended up with 15 principal components for SNA, 6 for METRICS, and 20 for the combined set of measures SNA+METRICS. The principal components were then used as the independent variables in the linear and logistic regression models.

5.2.3.2 Training Regression Models

To evaluate the predictive power of graph complexities we use a standard evaluation technique: *data splitting* (Munson and Khoshgoftaar, 1992). That is, we randomly pick two-thirds of all binaries to build a prediction model and use the remaining one-third to measure the efficacy of the built model (see Figure 5.4). For every experiment, we performed 50 random splits to ensure the stability and repeatability of our results—in total we trained 300 models. Whenever possible, we reused the random splits to facilitate comparison of results.

We measured the quality of *trained* models with:

- The **R^2 value** is the ratio of the regression sum of squares to the total sum of squares. It takes values between 0 and 1, with larger values indicating more variability explained by the model and less unexplained variation—a high R^2 value indicates good explanative power, but *not* predictive power. For logistic regression models, a specialized R^2 value introduced by Nagelkerke (1991) is typically used.

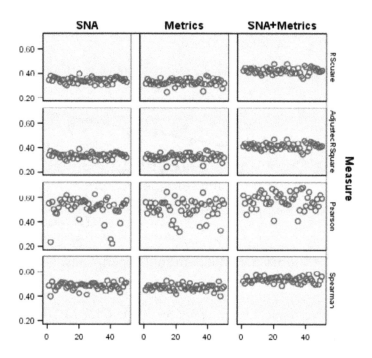

Figure 5.5: Results for linear regression.

- The **adjusted R^2 measure** also can be used to evaluate how well a model fits a given data set (Abreu and Melo, 1996). It explains for any bias in the R^2 measure by taking into account the degrees of freedom of the independent variables and the sample population. The adjusted R^2 tends to remain constant as the R^2 measure for large population samples.

Additionally, we performed **F-tests** on the regression models. Such tests measure the statistical significance of a model based on the null hypothesis that its regression coefficients are zero. In our case, every model was significant at 99%.

5.2.3.3   Linear Regression

In order to test how well linear regression models predict defects, we computed the Pearson and Spearman correlation coefficients (see Section 5.2.2) between the predicted number of defects and the actual number of defects. As before, the closer a value to –1 or +1, the higher two measures are correlated—in our case values close to 1 are desirable. In Figures 5.5 and 5.6, we report only correlations significant at 99%.

Figure 5.5 shows the results of the three experiments (SNA, METRICS, and the combination SNA+METRICS) for linear regression modeling, each of them with 50 random splits. For all three experiments, we observe consistent R^2 and adjusted R^2 values. This indicates the efficacy of the models built using the random split technique. The values for Pearson are less consistent; still we can observe high correlations (above 0.60).

The values for Spearman correlation values indicate the sensitivity of the predictions to estimate defects—i.e., an increase/decrease in the estimated values is accompanied by a corresponding increase/decrease in the actual number of defects. In all three experiments (SNA, METRICS, SNA+METRICS), the values for Spearman correlation are consistent across the 50 random splits. For SNA and METRICS separately the correlations are close to 0.50. This means that models built from network measures can predict defects as well as models built from complexity metrics. Building combined models increases the quality of the predictions, which is expressed by the correlations close to 0.60 in the SNA+METRICS experiment.

5.2.3.4   Binary Logistic Regression

We repeated our experiments using binary logistic regression model. In contrast to linear regression, logistic regression predicts likelihoods between 0 and 1. In our case, they can be interpreted as defect-proneness, i.e., the likelihood that a binary contains at least one defect. For training, we used the *sign(number of defects)* as dependent variable.

$$sign(number\ of\ defects) = \begin{cases} 1, & if\ number\ of\ defects > 0 \\ 0, & if\ number\ of\ defects = 0 \end{cases}$$

For prediction, we used a threshold of 0.50, i.e., all binaries with a defect-proneness of less than 0.50 were predicted as defect-free, while binaries with a defect-proneness of at least 0.50 were predicted as defect-prone.

In order to test the logistic regression models, we computed precision and recall. To explain these two measures, we use the following contingency table.

		Observed	
		Defect-prone	Defect-free
Predicted	Defect-prone (≥ 0.5)	A	B
	Defect-free (<0.5)	C	D

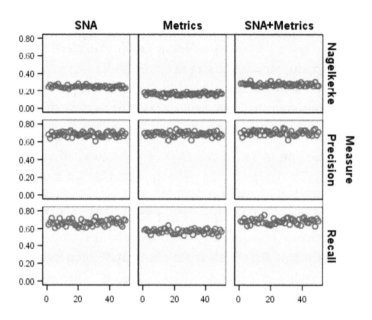

Figure 5.6: Results for logistic regression.

The *recall* $A/(A + C)$ measures the percentage of binaries *observed* as defect-prone that were classified correctly. The fewer false negatives (missed binaries), the closer the recall is to 1.

The *precision* $A/(A + B)$ measures the percentage of binaries percentage of binaries *predicted* as defect-prone that were classified correctly. The fewer false positives (incorrectly predicted as defect-prone), the closer the precision is to 1.

Both precision and recall should be as close to the value 1 as possible (=no false negatives and no false positives). However, such values are difficult to realize since precision and recall counteract each other.

Figure 5.6 shows the precision and recall values of the three experiments (SNA, METRICS, and SNA+METRICS) for logistic regression modeling. For each experiment, the values were consistent across the 50 random splits. The precision was around 0.70 in all three experiments. The recall was close to 0.60 for complexity metrics (METRICS), and close to 0.70 for the model built from network measures (SNA) and the combined model that used both complexity metrics and network measures (SNA+METRICS). These numbers show that network measures increase the recall by 0.10.

The results for both linear and logistic regression support our hypothesis, that *network measures on dependency graphs, can predict the number of post-release defects (H3).*

5.2.4 The Domino Effect

In 1975, Randell defined the domino effect principle (Randell, 1975):

> *"Given an arbitrary set of interacting processes, each with its own private recovery structure, a single error on the part of just one process could cause all the processes to use up many or even all of their recovery points, through a sort of uncontrolled domino effect."*

Restating Randell on dependency relationships, we hypothesize that defects in one component can significantly increase the likelihood of defects (in other words the probability of defects) in dependent components. This is a significant issue in understanding the cause-effect relationship of defects and the potential risk of propagating a defect through the entire system.

In order to identify critical binaries in Windows Server 2003, we investigated the distribution of the conditional likelihood $p(DEFECT \mid Binary\ depends\ on\ B)$ that a binary that directly depends on B has an associated defect.

$$p(DEFECT \mid Binary\ depends\ on\ B) =$$
$$\frac{\text{number of binaries that depend on B and have a defect}}{\text{number of binaries that depend on B}} \qquad (5.1)$$

Figure 5.7 shows an example (these numbers do not reflect actual values; they are just for illustrative purposes). There are three binaries that depend directly on B. Out of these three, two have defects; thus the above likelihood of defects is

$$p(DEFECT \mid Binary\ depends\ on\ B) = 2/3 = 0.66.$$

We also computed the likelihood of defects for additional distances, taking binaries into account that do not directly depend on B, but are two or more steps away. In Figure 5.7, four binaries indirectly depend on B over one intermediate step (distance $d = 2$), two of them have observed defects, thus the likelihood decreases to 0.50. In the same way, five binaries depend on B over two intermediate steps (distance $d = 3$), two of them have defects, thus the likelihood further decreases to 0.40. Our hypothesis is that binaries (closer to and) having dependencies on binaries with defects have a higher likelihood to contain defects.

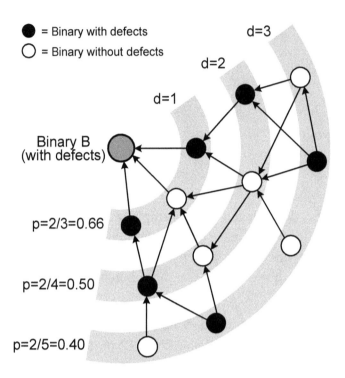

Figure 5.7: Computing likelihood of defects for binaries that depend on binary B (with distances d=1,2,3).

We divided the 2252 binaries of Windows Server 2003 into two categories, (i) binaries that contain defects and (ii) binaries that do not contain defects. For each of these categories we computed the probability that the neighboring binaries (d = 1,2,3) contain defects or not using Equation 5.1. We show the distribution of the likelihood of defects when depending on binaries *without* defects in Figure 5.8 and when depending on binaries *with* defects in Figure 5.9. To protect proprietary information, we anonymized the y-axis which reports the frequencies. Having the highest bar on the left (at 0.00), means that for most binaries the dependent binaries had no defects; the highest bar on the right (at 1.00X), shows that for most binaries all dependent binaries had defects.

In Figure 5.8, we show the distribution of $p(DEFECT \mid Binary\ depends\ on\ B)$ when depending on **binaries without defects**. For $d = 1$, we can observe that binaries can depend safely on every second binary without defects. In most cases when depending was not safe, there was only one depended binary which also had defects, thus resulting in a likelihood of 1.00 (as shown on the right side of the frequency bar chart for $d = 1$).

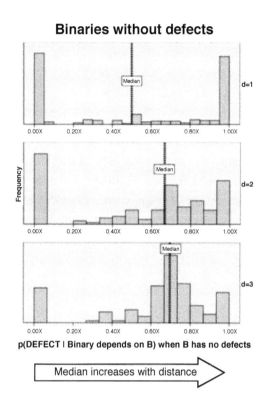

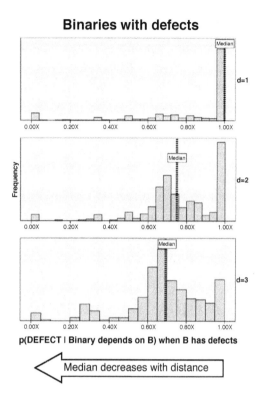

Figure 5.8: Distribution of likelihood of defects when depending on defect-free binaries.

Figure 5.9: Distribution of likelihood of defects when depending on defect-prone binaries.

We can also observe that when increasing the distance d, the median of the likelihood increases as well (trend towards the right). This means that being far away from binaries without defects increases the chances to fail. This could also be a due to the fact that as we move further away from a binary without defects we could become closer to other binaries with defects.

In contrast, Figure 5.9 shows the distribution of the likelihood when depending on **binaries with defects**. We see that directly depending on binaries with defects causes most binaries to have defects, too ($d = 1$). This effect decreases when the distance d increases (trend towards the left). In other words, we can observe a *domino effect*; however with every step it takes, its power (or likelihood) decreases. This trend is demonstrated by the shifting of the median from right to left with respect to the likelihood on depending on binaries with defects.

To summarize, the outliers in the opposite directions of Figure 5.8 and 5.9 clearly supports our hypothesis that, *depending on certain binaries correlates with the increase/decrease in the likelihood of observing a defect in a binary (H4).* This information can be very useful when making new design decisions to choose whether dependencies should be created on existing binaries with/without defects and located how far away from them.

The results also provide an empirical quantification of the domino effect on defects. As with all empirical studies there is always a degree of unknown variability, for example this could be an effect of the organizational structure of Windows, the working level and experience (or lack thereof) of the developers, the complexity of the code base, or the extent of churn in the code base.

5.3 Threats to Validity

In this section we discuss the threats to validity of our work. We assumed that fixes occur in the same location as the corresponding defect. Although this is not always true, this assumption is frequently used in research (Fenton and Ohlsson, 2000; Möller and Paulish, 1993; Nagappan et al., 2006b; Ostrand et al., 2005). As stated by Basili et al., drawing general conclusions from empirical studies in software engineering is difficult because any process depends on a potentially large number of relevant context variables (Basili et al., 1999). For this reason, we cannot assume a priori that the results of a study generalize beyond the specific environment in which it was conducted.

Since this study was performed on the Windows operating system and the size of the code base and development organization is at a much larger scale than many commercial products, it is likely that the specific models built for Windows would not apply to other products, even those built by Microsoft.

This previous threat in particular is frequently misunderstood as a criticism on empirical studies. Another common misinterpretation is that nothing new learned from the result of empirical studies or more commonly "I already knew this result". Unfortunately, some readers miss the fact that this wisdom has rarely been shown to be true and is often quoted without scientific evidence. Further, data on defects is rare and replication is a common empirical research practice. We are confident that dependency data has predictive power for other projects—we will repeat our experiments for other Microsoft products and invite everyone to do the same for other software projects.

5.4 Summary

We showed that network measures on dependency graphs predict defects for binaries of Windows Server 2003. This supports managers in the task of allocating resources such as time and cost for quality assurance. Ideally, the parts with most defects would be tested most.

The results of this empirical study are as follows.

- Complexity metrics fail to predict binaries that developers consider as critical (only 30% are predicted; Section 5.2.1).

- Network measures can predict 60% of these critical binaries (Section 5.2.1).

- Network measures on dependency graphs can indicate and predict the number of defects (Sections 5.2.2 and 5.2.3).

- When used for classification, network measures have a recall that is 0.10 higher than for complexity metrics with a comparable precision (Section 5.2.3).

- We observed a domino effect in Windows Server 2003: depending on defect-prone binaries increases the chances of having defects (Section 5.2.4).

6

Predicting Defects for Subsystems

In this chapter, we will investigate whether dependency data predicts defects. Rather than using code complexity metrics for individual binaries, we will compute complexity measures for the dependency graphs of whole subsystems. By using graph theoretic properties we can take the interaction between binaries into account. Formally, our research hypotheses are the following.

H1 *For subsystems, the complexity of dependency graphs positively correlates with the number of post-release defects*—an increase in complexity is accompanied by an increase in defects.

H2 *The complexity of dependency graphs can predict the number of post-release defects.*

H3 *The quality of the predictions improves when they are made for subsystems that are higher in the system's architecture.*

The outline of this chapter is as follows. First, we will present the data collection for our study (Section 6.1). In our experiments, we evaluated how well the complexity of a subsystem's dependency graph predict the number of defects (Section 6.2). We close with a discussion of threats to validity (Section 6.3).

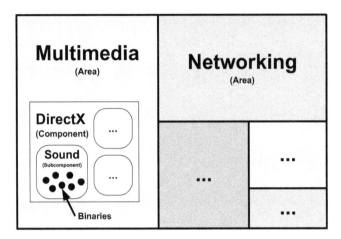

Figure 6.1: Example architecture of Windows Server 2003.

6.1 Data Collection

In this section, we explain how we collected hierarchy information and software dependencies and how we measured the complexity of subsystems. For our experiments we used the Windows Server 2003 operating system which is decomposed into a hierarchy of subsystems as shown in Figure 6.1. On the highest level are *areas* such as "Multimedia" or "Networking". Areas are further decomposed into *components* such as "Multimedia: DirectX" (DirectX is a Windows technology that enables higher performance in graphics and sound when users are playing games or watching video on their PC) and *subcomponents* such as "Multimedia: DirectX: Sound". On the lowest level are the *binaries* to which we can accurately map defects; we considered post-release defects because they matter most for end-users. Since defects are mapped to the level of binaries, we can aggregate the defect counts of the binaries of a subsystem *(areas, components, subcomponents)* to get its total subsystem defect count.

We first generate a dependency graph for Windows Server 2003 at the level of binaries (Section 6.1.1). Then we divide this graph into different kinds of subgraphs using the area/component/subcomponent hierarchy (Section 6.1.2). For the subgraphs, we compute complexity measures (Section 6.1.3) which we finally use to predict defects for subsystems. We placed our analysis on the level of binaries for two reasons: (i) Binaries are easier to analyze since one is independent from the build process and other specialties such as preprocessors. (ii) Defects were collected on binary level; mapping them back to source code is challenging and might distort our study.

6.1.1 Software Dependencies

For the computation of software dependencies, we refer to Section 5.1.1. To recall, a dependency graph is a directed multigraph $G_M = (V, A)$ where

- V is a set of nodes (binaries) and
- $A = (E, m)$ a multiset of edges (dependencies) for which $E \subseteq V \times V$ contains the actual edges and the function $m : E \to N$ returns the multiplicity (count) of an edge.

The corresponding regular graph (without multiedges) is $G = (V, E)$. We allow self-edges for both regular graphs and multigraphs. For the experiments in this Section, we will consider both regular graphs (where only one edge between two binaries is counted) and multigraphs (where every edge between two binaries is counted).

6.1.2 Dependency Subgraphs

We use hierarchy data from Windows Server 2003 to split the dependency graph $G_M = (V, A)$ into several subgraphs; for a subsystem that consists of binaries B, we compute the following subgraphs (see also Figure 6.2):

Intra-dependencies (INTRA). The subgraph (V_{intra}, E_{intra}) contains all the *intra-dependencies*, i.e., dependencies (u, v) that exist between two binaries $u, v \in B$ within the subsystem. This subgraph is induced by the set of binaries B that are part of the subsystem.

$$V_{intra} = B$$
$$E_{intra} = \{(u, v) \mid (u, v) \in E, u \in B, v \in B\}$$
$$A_{intra} = (E_{intra}, m)$$

Outgoing dependencies (OUT). The subgraph (V_{out}, E_{out}) contains all *outgoing* inter-dependencies (u, v) that connect the subsystem with other subsystems, i.e., $u \in B$, $v \notin B$. This subgraph is induced by the set of edges that represent outgoing dependencies. We focus on outgoing dependencies because they are the ones that can make code fail.

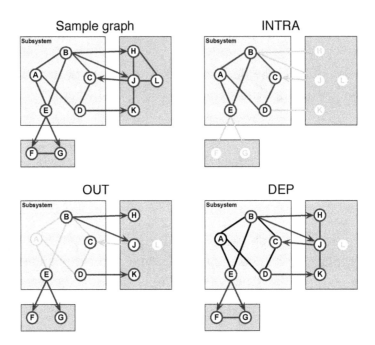

Figure 6.2: Different subgraphs for a subsystem that consists of binaries A, B, C, D, and E: intra-dependency (INTRA), outgoing dependency (OUT), and combined dependency graph (DEP).

$$E_{out} = \{(u,v) \mid (u,v) \in E, u \in B, v \notin B\}$$
$$V_{out} = \{u \mid (u,v) \in E_{out}\} \cup \{v \mid (u,v) \in E_{out}\}$$
$$A_{out} = (E_{out}, m)$$

Subsystem dependency graph (DEP). The subgraph (V_{dep}, E_{dep}) combines the intra-dependencies and the outgoing dependencies subgraphs. Note that we additionally take edges between the neighbors of the subsystem into account.

$$V_{dep} = V_{intra} \cup V_{out}$$
$$E_{dep} = \{(u,v) \mid (u,v) \in E, u \in V_{dep}, v \in V_{dep}\}$$
$$A_{dep} = (E_{intra}, m)$$

Considering different subgraphs allows us to investigate the influence of internal vs. external dependencies on post-release defects. We compute the dependencies across all the three subsystem levels (area, component, and subcomponent).

6.1.3   Graph-Theoretic Complexity Measures

On the subgraphs defined in the previous section, we compute complexity measures which we will later use to predict post-release defects. The complexity measures are computed for both regular graph and multigraphs with the main difference being the number of edges E and $\sum_{e \in E} m(e)$ respectively. Some of the measures are aggregated from values for nodes and edges by using minimum, maximum and average.

The formulas are summarized in Table 6.1 and discussed below.

Graph complexity.   Besides simple complexity measures such as the *number of nodes* or *number of edges*, we compute the *graph complexity* and the *density* of a graph (West, 2001). Although the graph complexity was developed for graphs in general, it is well known in software engineering for its use on control flow graphs (Mc-Cabe's cyclomatic complexity).

Degree-based complexity.   We count the number of ingoing and outgoing edges (degree) of nodes and aggregate them by using minimum, maximum, and average. These values allow us to investigate whether the aggregated number of dependencies has an impact on defects.

Distance-based complexity.   By using the Floyd-Warshall algorithm (Cormen et al., 2001), we compute the shortest distance between all pairs of nodes. For regular graphs, the initial distance between two connected nodes is 1. For multigraphs, we assume that the higher the multiplicity of an edge e, the closer the incident nodes are to each other; thus we set the initial distance to $1/m(e)$. From the distances we compute the *eccentricity* of a node v which is the greatest distance between v and any other node. We aggregate all eccentricities with minimum (=radius), maximum (=diameter), and average. With distance-based complexities we can investigate if the propagation of dependencies has an impact on defects.

Multiplicity-based complexity.   For multigraphs, we measure the minimum, maximum and average multiplicity of edges. This also allows us to investigate the relation between number of dependencies and defects.

Table 6.1: Complexity measures for a multigraph $G_M = (V, (E, m))$ and its underlying graph $G = (V, E)$. The set of *weakly* connected components is P; $in(v)$ returns the ingoing and $out(v)$ the outgoing edges of a node v.

	Regular graph	Multigraph	Aggregation
Number of NODES	$|V|$	$|V|$	Not necessary
Number of EDGES	$|E|$	$\sum_{e \in E} m(e)$	Not necessary
COMPLEXITY	$|E| - |V| + |P|$	$\sum_{e \in E} m(e) - |V| + |P|$	Not necessary
DENSITY	$\dfrac{|E|}{|V| \cdot |V|}$	$\dfrac{\sum_{e \in E} m(e)}{|V| \cdot |V|}$	Not necessary
DEGREE of node v	$|in(v) \cup out(v)|$	$\sum_{e \in in(v) \cup out(v)} m(e)$	Over nodes $v \epsilon V$ using min, max, avg.
ECCENTRICITY of node v	max{dist(v, w)|wϵV}	max{multidist(v, w)|wϵV}	Over nodes $v \epsilon V$ using min, max, avg.
MULTIPLICITY of edge e	1	$m(e)$	Over edges $e \epsilon E$ using min, max, avg.

6.2 Experimental Analysis

In this section, we will support our hypotheses that complexity of dependency graphs predicts the number of defects for a subsystem, with several experiments. We carried out the experiments on three different architecture levels of Windows Server 2003: subcomponents, components, and areas. We will mostly focus on the *subcomponent* level. We start with a correlation analysis of complexity measures and number of defects (Section 6.2.1) and continue with building regression models for defect prediction (Section 6.2.2). Next, we summarize the results for the *component* and *area* levels and discuss the influence of granularity (Section 6.2.3).

6.2.1 Correlation Analysis

In order to investigate our initial hypothesis H1, we determined the Pearson and Spearman rank correlation between the dependency graph complexities measures for each subcomponent (Sections 6.1.2 and 6.1.3) and its number of defects. For Pearson correlation to be applied the data requires a linear distribution, Spearman rank correlation can even be applied for non-linear associations between values (Fenton and Pfleeger, 1998). The closer the value of correlation is to −1 or +1, the higher two measures are correlated—positively for +1 and negatively for −1.

The results for subcomponent level of Windows Server 2003 are shown in Table 6.2. The table shows the complexity measures in the rows (Section 6.1.3) and the different kinds of dependency graphs in the columns (Section 6.1.2). Correlations that are significant at 0.99 are indicated with (*); note that the *Multi_Edges* and *Multi_Complexity* measures were strongly inter-correlated, which resulted in almost the same correlations with the number of defects. For space reasons we omit we the inter-correlations between the complexity measures. The correlation for the area and component level can be found in Table 6.3 and 6.4.

In Table 6.2 we can make the following observations.

(O1) For most measures the correlations are significant (indicated by *) and positive. This means that with an increase of such measures there an increase in the number of defects, though at different levels of strength.

(O2) The only notable negative correlation is for *Density*, which means that with an increase in the density of dependencies there is a decrease in the number of defects. This effect is strongest for DEP graphs. When taking multiedges into account (*Multi_Density*) the effect vanishes.

(O3) When we neglect multiplicity and consider *only presence of dependencies*, we obtain the highest correlations for subgraphs that additionally contain the neighborhood of a subsystem (DEP).

(O4) When we take *multiplicity* of dependencies into account the correlations are highest for subgraphs that contain only dependencies within the subsystem (INTRA).

(O5) The correlations are highest for the two inter-correlated measures *Multi_Edges* and *Multi_Complexity*, and for *Multi_Degree_Max* and *Multi_Multiplicity_Max* (highlighted in **bold**). All of these measures consider multiedges, suggesting that the number of dependencies matters and not just the presence.

To summarize we could observe significant correlations for most complexity measures, and most of them were positive and high (O1, O5). This confirms our initial hypothesis that *the complexity of dependency graphs positively correlates with the number of post-release defects (H1)*. The only exception we observed was the density of a dependency graph (O2). This is surprising, especially since cliques tend to have a high

Table 6.2: Correlation values between the number of defects and complexity measures (on subcomponent level).

		Pearson				Spearman			
		INTRA	OUT	DEP		INTRA	OUT	DEP	
NODES		.325(*)	.497(*)	.501(*)	O3	.338(*)	.579(*)	.580(*)	O3
EDGES		.321(*)	.454(*)	.485(*)		.353(*)	.586(*)	.567(*)	
COMPLEXITY		.319(*)	.322(*)	.481(*)		.346(*)	.387(*)	.564(*)	
DENSITY	O2	-.312(*)	-.292(*)	-.418(*)		-.294(*)	-.506(*)	-.519(*)	
DEGREE_MIN		.168(*)	.054	.014		.182(*)	.030	.145(*)	
DEGREE_MAX		.332(*)	.409(*)	.496(*)		.347(*)	.533(*)	.569(*)	
DEGREE_AVG		.386(*)	.377(*)	.366(*)		.332(*)	.516(*)	.526(*)	
ECCENTRICITY_MIN		.293(*)	.164(*)	.009		.314(*)	.305(*)	.079	
ECCENTRICITY_MAX		.307(*)	.201(*)	.094(*)		.323(*)	.337(*)	.370(*)	
ECCENTRICITY_AVG		.303(*)	.193(*)	.099(*)		.317(*)	.471(*)	.527(*)	
MULTI_EDGES	O4	.728(*)	.432(*)	.393(*)	O4	.667(*)	.671(*)	.524(*)	
MULTI_COMPLEXITY		.728(*)	.432(*)	.393(*)		.667(*)	.671(*)	.524(*)	
MULTI_DENSITY		.290(*)	.116(*)	-.108(*)		.455(*)	.282(*)	-.138(*)	
MULTI_DEGREE_MIN		.376(*)	.006	.177(*)		.296(*)	-.298(*)	.045	
MULTI_DEGREE_MAX		.637(*)	.395(*)	.356(*)		.643(*)	.654(*)	.511(*)	
MULTI_DEGREE_AVG		.538(*)	.247(*)	.148(*)		.597(*)	.597(*)	.364(*)	
MULTI_MULTIPLICITY_MIN		.300(*)	.005	-.020		.201(*)	-.355(*)	-.328(*)	
MULTI_MULTIPLICITY_MAX		.640(*)	.389(*)	.249(*)		.640(*)	.634(*)	.418(*)	
MULTI_MULTIPLICITY_AVG		.454(*)	.178(*)	.013		.571(*)	.505(*)	.102(*)	
MULTI_ECCENTRICITY_MIN		.267(*)	.136(*)	-.010		.311(*)	.313(*)	.015	
MULTI_ECCENTRICITY_MAX		.267(*)	.141(*)	-.010		.312(*)	.346(*)	.060	
MULTI_ECCENTRICITY_AVG		.267(*)	.137(*)	-.010		.311(*)	.302(*)	.016	

defect-proneness (see Section 2) and a high density at the same time. One possible explanation for the poor correlation of density might be that normalizing the number of dependencies $|E|$ by the squared number of binaries $|V| \cdot |V|$ is too strong. This is supported by the *Degree_Avg* measure which normalizes $|E|$ only by $|V|$ and has a rather high positive correlation (up to 0.527 for Spearman).

The different results for complexity measures with and without multiplicity (O3 and O4), might suggest that one should consider both, the multiplicity of dependencies and the neighborhood of a subsystem—however, dependencies across subsystems should be weighted less. In future work, we will investigate whether this actually holds true.

Table 6.3: Correlation values between the number of defects and complexity measures (on component level).

	Pearson			Spearman		
	INTRA	OUT	DEP	INTRA	OUT	DEP
NODES	.679(*)	.729(*)	.735(*)	.653(*)	.730(*)	.743(*)
EDGES	.717(*)	.765(*)	.674(*)	.672(*)	.748(*)	.695(*)
COMPLEXITY	.718(*)	.723(*)	.664(*)	.668(*)	.660(*)	.681(*)
DENSITY	-.487(*)	-.350(*)	-.572(*)	-.584(*)	-.557(*)	-.740(*)
DEGREE_MIN	-.055	.001	-.302(*)	.023	.050	-.297(*)
DEGREE_MAX	.640(*)	.415(*)	.642(*)	.623(*)	.572(*)	.706(*)
DEGREE_AVG	.582(*)	.562(*)	.340(*)	.573(*)	.642(*)	.496(*)
ECCENTRICITY_MIN	.654(*)	.627(*)	.037	.603(*)	.516(*)	.346(*)
ECCENTRICITY_MAX	.660(*)	.639(*)	.106	.622(*)	.566(*)	.436(*)
ECCENTRICITY_AVG	.658(*)	.637(*)	.090	.612(*)	.628(*)	.692(*)
MULTI_EDGES	.691(*)	.327(*)	.428(*)	.724(*)	.635(*)	.545(*)
MULTI_COMPLEXITY	.691(*)	.327(*)	.428(*)	.724(*)	.635(*)	.545(*)
MULTI_DENSITY	-.034	-.108(*)	-.354(*)	-.045	.074	-.604(*)
MULTI_DEGREE_MIN	-.067	-.043	-.140(*)	-.213(*)	-.266(*)	-.367(*)
MULTI_DEGREE_MAX	.443(*)	.225(*)	.360(*)	.597(*)	.586(*)	.502(*)
MULTI_DEGREE_AVG	.147(*)	.054	-.227(*)	.400(*)	.496(*)	-.111(*)
MULTI_MULTIPLICITY_MIN	-.072	-.041	-.043	-.356(*)	-.440(*)	-.449(*)
MULTI_MULTIPLICITY_MAX	.426(*)	.189(*)	.193(*)	.580(*)	.535(*)	.324(*)
MULTI_MULTIPLICITY_AVG	.049	-.037	-.318(*)	.295(*)	.323(*)	-.395(*)
MULTI_ECCENTRICITY_MIN	.645(*)	.616(*)	-.026	.587(*)	.424(*)	.375(*)
MULTI_ECCENTRICITY_MAX	.645(*)	.618(*)	-.024	.588(*)	.467(*)	.418(*)
MULTI_ECCENTRICITY_AVG	.645(*)	.616(*)	-.026	.588(*)	.389(*)	.381(*)

Table 6.4: Correlation values between the number of defects and complexity measures (on area level).

	Pearson			Spearman		
	INTRA	OUT	DEP	INTRA	OUT	DEP
NODES	.906(*)	.942(*)	.935(*)	.916(*)	.911(*)	.921(*)
EDGES	.954(*)	.940(*)	.926(*)	.925(*)	.891(*)	.905(*)
COMPLEXITY	.949(*)	.921(*)	.916(*)	.924(*)	.862(*)	.904(*)
DENSITY	-.416(*)	-.552(*)	-.558(*)	-.850(*)	-.873(*)	-.905(*)
DEGREE_MIN	-.243(*)	.(a)	-.411(*)	-.285(*)	.	-.548(*)
DEGREE_MAX	.916(*)	.938(*)	.945(*)	.899(*)	.890(*)	.919(*)
DEGREE_AVG	.580(*)	.446(*)	.297(*)	.765(*)	.733(*)	.582(*)
ECCENTRICITY_MIN	.897(*)	.819(*)	.757(*)	.844(*)	.642(*)	.518(*)
ECCENTRICITY_MAX	.898(*)	.822(*)	.760(*)	.863(*)	.683(*)	.567(*)
ECCENTRICITY_AVG	.898(*)	.821(*)	.759(*)	.856(*)	.685(*)	.741(*)
MULTI_EDGES	.836(*)	.711(*)	.694(*)	.913(*)	.843(*)	.835(*)
MULTI_COMPLEXITY	.836(*)	.711(*)	.694(*)	.913(*)	.843(*)	.835(*)
MULTI_DENSITY	-.127	-.164	-.455(*)	-.396(*)	-.224	-.849(*)
MULTI_DEGREE_MIN	-.109	-.117	-.103	-.612(*)	-.476(*)	-.601(*)
MULTI_DEGREE_MAX	.395(*)	.680(*)	.661(*)	.795(*)	.822(*)	.802(*)
MULTI_DEGREE_AVG	.118	.077	-.441(*)	.530(*)	.548(*)	-.435(*)
MULTI_MULTIPLICITY_MIN	-.097	-.175	-.428(*)	-.737(*)	-.711(*)	-.669(*)
MULTI_MULTIPLICITY_MAX	.328(*)	.194	.336(*)	.788(*)	.670(*)	.624(*)
MULTI_MULTIPLICITY_AVG	-.027	-.044	-.511(*)	.281(*)	.421(*)	-.653(*)
MULTI_ECCENTRICITY_MIN	.896(*)	.816(*)	.752(*)	.828(*)	.637(*)	.541(*)
MULTI_ECCENTRICITY_MAX	.896(*)	.817(*)	.753(*)	.828(*)	.688(*)	.547(*)
MULTI_ECCENTRICITY_AVG	.896(*)	.817(*)	.752(*)	.828(*)	.605(*)	.535(*)

6.2.2 Regression Analysis

So since complexity of dependency graphs correlates with post-release defects, can we use complexity to predict defects? To answer this question, we build multiple linear regression (MLR) models where the number of post-release defects forms the dependent variable and our complexity measures form the independent variables. We build separate models for every type of subgraph (INTRA, OUT, and DEP) and a combined model that uses all measures from Table 6.2 as independent variables (COMBINED). We carried out 24 experiments: one for each combination out of two kinds of regression (linear, logistic), three granularities (areas, components, subcomponents,) and four different sets of complexities (INTRA, OUT, DEP, COMBINED).

However, one difficulty associated with MLR is multicollinearity among the independent variables. Multicollinearity comes from inter-correlations such as between the aforementioned *Multi_Edges* and *Multi_Complexity*. Inter-correlations can lead to an inflated variance in the estimation of the dependent variable. To overcome this problem, we use a standard statistical approach called *Principal Component Analysis* (PCA) (Jackson, 2003). With PCA, a small number of uncorrelated linear combinations of variables are selected for use in regression (linear or logistic). These combinations are independent and thus do not suffer from multicollinearity, while at the same time they account for as much sample variance as possible—for our experiments we selected principal components that account for a cumulative sample variance greater than 95%. We ended up with 5 principal components for INTRA, 7 for OUT, 6 for DEP, and 14 for the COMBINED set of measures. The principal components are then used as the independent variables.

To evaluate the predictive power of graph complexities we use a standard evaluation technique: *data splitting* (Munson and Khoshgoftaar, 1992). That is, we randomly pick two-thirds of all binaries to build a prediction model and use the remaining one-third to measure the efficacy of the built model. For every experiment, we performed 50 random splits to ensure the stability and repeatability of our results—in total we trained 1200 models. Whenever possible, we reused the random splits to facilitate comparison.

We measured the quality of *trained* models with:

- The **R^2 value** is the ratio of the regression sum of squares to the total sum of squares. It takes values between 0 and 1, with larger values indicating more variability explained by the model and less unexplained variation—a high R^2 value indicates good explanative power, but *not* predictive power.

- The **adjusted R^2 measure** also can be used to evaluate how well a model fits a given data set (Abreu and Melo, 1996). It explains for any bias in the R^2 measure by taking into account the degrees of freedom of the independent variables and the sample population. The adjusted R^2 tends to remain constant as the R^2 measure for large population samples.

Additionally, we performed **F-tests** on the regression models. Such tests measure the statistical significance of a model based on the null hypothesis that its regression coefficients are zero. In our case, every model was significant at 99%.

For *testing*, we measured the predictive power with the Pearson and Spearman correlation coefficients. The Spearman rank correlation is a commonly-used robust correlation technique (Fenton and Pfleeger, 1998) because it can be applied even when the association between elements is non-linear; the Pearson bivariate correlation requires the data to be distributed normally and the association between elements to be linear. For completeness we compute the Pearson correlations also. As before, the closer the value of a correlation is to –1 or +1, the higher two measures are correlated—in our case we are correlating the predicted number of defects with the actual number of defects (for MLR); and defect-proneness probabilities with actual number of defects (logistic regression), thus values close to 1 are desirable. In Figures 6 to 8, we report only correlations that were significant at 99%.

Linear regression

Figure 6.3 shows the results of four experiments on subcomponent level for linear regression modeling, each of them consisting of 50 random splits. Except for OUT graphs, we can observe the consistent R^2 and adjusted R^2 values. This indicates the efficacy of the models built using the random split technique.

The values for Pearson are less consistent, still we can observe high correlations, especially for INTRA and COMBINED (around 0.70).

The values for Spearman correlation (0.60) are very consistent and highest for OUT and COMBINED subgraphs. These values indicate the sensitivity of the predictions to estimate defects—that is an increase/decrease in the estimated values is accompanied by a corresponding increase/decrease in the actual number of defects.

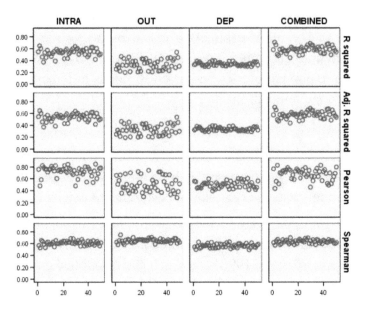

Figure 6.3: Results for linear regression.

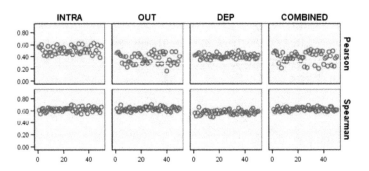

Figure 6.4: Results for logistic regression.

Binary logistic regression

We repeated our experiments with the same 50 random splits using a binary logistic regression model. In contrast to linear regression, logistic regression predicts a value between 0 and 1. This value can be interpreted as defect-proneness, i.e., the likelihood to contain at least one defect. Figure 6.4 shows the results of our random split experiments. All results are consistent, except the Pearson values.

Compared to linear regression, the Pearson correlations are lower because the relation between predicted defect-proneness and actual number of defects is obviously not linear. Thus, using logistic regression did not make much difference in our case. Still, the results for both linear and logistic regression support our hypothesis, that *the complexity of dependency graphs can predict the number of post-release defects (H2)*.

6.2.3 Granularity

The previous results were for the subcomponent level. Figure 6.5 shows how the results for linear regression change when we make predictions for component and area level. We can observe that for both the maxima of correlation increases: for Pearson up to 0.927 (components) and 0.992 (areas); for Spearman up to 0.877 (components) and 0.961 (areas). While for component level the results are stable, we can observe many fluctuations for area level.

To summarize, the results for component level show that *the quality of the predictions improves when they are made for subsystems that are higher in the system's architecture (H3)*—the results for area level also support this hypothesis, however, they additionally demonstrate that the gain in predictive power can come with a decreased stability. Thus it is important to find a good balance between the granularity of reliable predictions and stability.

6.3 Threats to Validity

In this section we discuss the threats to validity of our work. We assumed that fixes occur in the same location as the corresponding defect. Although this is not always true, this assumption is frequently used in research (Fenton and Ohlsson, 2000; Möller and Paulish, 1993; Nagappan et al., 2006b; Ostrand et al., 2005). As stated by Basili et al., drawing general conclusions from empirical studies in software engineering is difficult because any process depends on a potentially large number of relevant context variables (Basili et al., 1999). For this reason, we cannot assume a priori that the results of a study generalize beyond the specific environment in which it was conducted.

Since this study was performed on the Windows operating system and the size of the code base and development organization is at a much larger scale than many commercial products, it is likely that the specific models built for Windows would not apply

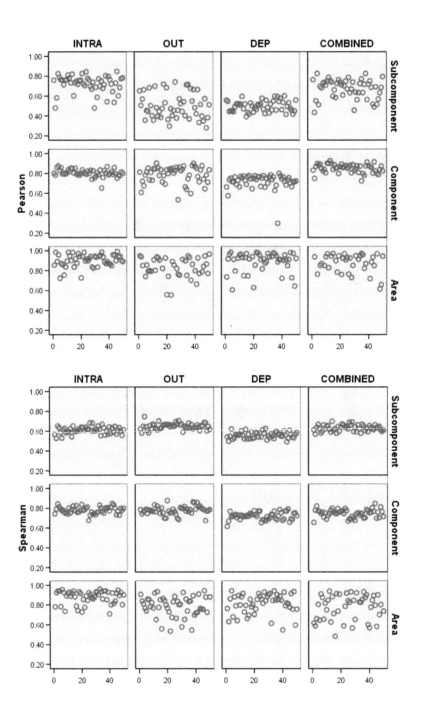

Figure 6.5: Correlations for different levels of granularity

to other products, even those built by Microsoft. This threat in particular is frequently misunderstood as a criticism on empirical studies. However, data on defects is rare and a common empirical research practice is to carry out studies for one project and replicate them on others. However, we are confident that dependency data has predictive power for other projects—we will repeat our experiments for other Microsoft products and invite everyone to do the same for other software.

6.4 Summary

We showed that for subsystems, one can use the complexity of dependency graphs for predicting defects. This helps for resource allocation and decision making. With respect to this, our lessons learned are as follows.

- Most dependency graph complexities can predict the number of defects (Sections 6.2.1 and 6.2.2).

- Validate any complexity measure before using it for decisions (Section 6.2.1).

- Find a balance between the granularity, reliability, and stability of predictions (Section 6.2.3).

6.5 Discussion

We do not claim that dependency data is the sole predictor of post-release defects—however, our results are another piece in the *puzzle of why software fails*. Other effective predictors include code complexity metrics (Nagappan et al., 2006b) and process metrics like code churn (Nagappan and Ball, 2005). In our future work, we will identify more predictors and work on assembling the pieces of the puzzle. Also we plan to look at more non-linear regression and other machine learning techniques. More specifically, we will focus on the following topics.

Evolution of dependencies. We will apply the concept of churn to dependencies. More precisely, we plan to compare the dependencies of different Windows releases to identify *churned dependencies* and investigate their relation to defects.

Development process. How can we include the development process in our predictions? There are many *different characteristics* to describe the process, ranging from size of personnel to criticality, dynamism, and culture (Boehm and Turner, 2003). How much difference do agile and plan-driven development processes make with respect to defects? And how much impact has global development?

The human factor. Last but not least, humans are the ones who introduce defects. How can we include the *human factor* (Ko and Myers, 2005) into predictions about future defects? This will be a challenge for both software engineering and human computer interaction—and ultimately it will reveal why programmers fail and show ways how to avoid it.

Part III

Synopsis

7

Conclusion

Software development results in a huge amount of data: changes to source code are recorded in version archives, bugs are reported to issue tracking systems, and communications are archived in e-mails and newsgroups. Mining software repositories makes use all of this data to understand and support software development. This book makes the following contributions to this area.

Fine-grained analysis of version archives. The work on mining usage patterns was the first to analyze particular code changes and not only the changed location. DYNAMINE learned *project-specific usage pattern of methods* from version archives and validated the patterns with dynamic program analysis, which is another novelty. (Chapter 2)

The aspect-mining tool HAM reveals *cross-cutting changes*: "A developer invoked lock() and unlock() in 1,284 different locations." In aspect-oriented programming, such changes can be encapsulated as aspects. By breaking down large code-bases into their evolution steps, HAM scales to large systems such as Eclipse. (Chapter 3)

Mining bug databases to predict defects. In software development, resources for quality assurance (QA) are typically limited. A common practice among managers is *resource allocation* that is to direct the QA effort to those parts of a system that are expected to have most defects.

This book presented techniques to build models that can successfully predict the most defect-prone parts of large-scale industrial software, in our experiments Windows Server 2003. The proposed measures on dependency graphs outperformed traditional complexity metrics. In addition, we found empirical evidence for a domino effect: *depending on defect-prone binaries increases the chances of having defects.* (Chapters 5 and 6)

Dependencies between subsystems are typically define early in the design phase; thus, designers can easily explore and assess design alternatives in terms of expected quality.

Mining software repositories works best on large projects with a long and rich development history; smaller and new projects, however, rarely have enough data for the above techniques. Our future work, will therefore focus on *mining software repositories across projects.* We hypothesize that projects which do not have enough history can learn from the repositories shared by other similar projects. For instance, open-source communities (such as SourceForge.net) host several thousand projects, which are all available for mining. Similarly, within an industrial setting, companies can learn from all their ongoing and completed projects.

Having access to the history of other projects supports developers and managers to make well-informed decisions, for instance with respect to design ("Which library should we use?"), personnel ("Who is qualified for this task?"), and resource allocation ("What parts should we test most?"). They can identify similar situations in the past, and see how these situations impacted the evolution of a project. Overall, the goal is to automate most of this process and provide appropriate tool support for both open- and closed-source software development.

On the one hand, we expect that existing mining techniques will benefit from a *larger population* of projects. For instance, change classification frequently finds insufficient evidence within a single project to blame bad changes, which results in a large number of false negatives (Kim et al., 2006). By extending the search space to many projects, we are more likely to find enough evidence. We can also *transfer knowledge* from one project to another similar project. Nagappan et al. (2006a) observed that defect prediction models trained on one project can reliably predict defects for projects with comparable development processes.

On the other hand, having access to many projects poses new research questions, one of them being: "What can we mine from such data in an automatic, large-scale (many projects), and tool-oriented fashion to support software development?" We will discuss some ideas below.

Risk assessment of libraries. By comparing the bug histories and evolution of projects, we can identify libraries that are risky to use (with respect to defects and complexity).

> *"The library openssl.jar adds about 42% more risk (defects) to your project than library cryptlib.jar, which provides similar functionality."*

Risk information helps developers to avoid "poisonous" libraries that increase defect count or complexity of a project. In past research, we empirically showed that the defect-proneness of a component can be defined by the classes that are imported (Schröter et al., 2006). As a next step we plan to identify defect-prone imports, aggregate the information to libraries, and identify libraries with similar functionality—all of this automatically for many projects.

In addition, we will annotate the risk assessment of libraries with problematic usages mined from software repositories. This information makes developers aware of potential pitfalls and helps them to avoid repeating mistakes made by other developers (in other projects).

Recommending similar artifacts. By searching similar artifacts, we can help developers to retrieve information useful for modification tasks.

> *"The bug report at hand is similar to bug report #42233 in the Eclipse project."*

> *"The method parseFile() in your project is similar to parseXML() in the Ant project."*

The Hipikat (Cubranic et al., 2005) and CodeBroker (Ye and Fischer, 2002) tools provide such recommendations for single projects. In our research, we will extend these techniques to scale to a large number projects. We will focus especially on similarity between *different kinds of artifacts*. For instance, in order to correct a bug, a developer might want to search for source code or newsgroup discussions that are similar to the bug report.

Identification of experts – worldwide! By mining across projects, we can locate experts not only within a single project but also within thousands of projects.

"Erich is the best candidate to design and implement IDEs."

Past research identified experts for source code artifacts (such as classes or methods) as the developers who changed the artifact most frequently or most recently (McDonald and Ackerman, 2000; Mockus and Herbsleb, 2002).

We plan to provide information about expertise on a *social networking site* for developers. The site will help managers to recruit new team members ("Who has experience with the Eclipse AST parser?") and developers to identify colleagues with similar interests ("Who has similar expertise and what are they working on?").

Recommending emerging changes. By monitoring the evolution of thousands of projects, we can identify trends and recommend changes to developers.

"This unit test uses assert(); consider changing it to assertTrue()"

Assume that there are several fragments in which the calls to assert() have been changed to assertTrue(). If the code at hand still contains assert(), the programmer may make her code future-proof by applying the same renaming. This project generalizes the detection of refactorings (Weißgerber and Diehl, 2006) and change classification (Kim et al., 2006) to arbitrary changes. The identification of emerging changes (trends) is an additional challenge.

Timeline views of project evolution. By mining version control archives and bug databases, we can extracts key dates in the evolution of projects.

"February 24: Major refactorings of the server component.
April 9: The change 'new parser' increased the project's complexity by 42%."

In past research, we annotated charts depicting the evolution of documentation quality by connecting jumps with commit messages (Schreck et al., 2007). We want to extend this research by building a tool that automatically creates a timeline of key events of *one or more* projects. This timeline can include events known by developers, such as major refactorings (Weißgerber and Diehl, 2006) and architecture changes (Pinzger et al., 2005); however, we will focus on unnoticeable changes that still have a substantial impact on a project (as quantified by metrics such as complexity or documentation quality). Timelines of several projects can be combined to a news-feed and integrated in IDEs such as Jazz.Net.

At the beginning of the last century, the philosopher George Santayana remarked that those who could not remember the past would be condemned to repeat it. In other words, to achieve progress, we must learn from history. With our future research, everyone will get enough history from which to learn.

Acknowledgments

Thousand thanks to *Prof. Andreas Zeller* for his advise and continuous confidence in my work. All this work would not have been possible without his guidance and support. Very special thanks to *Prof. Harald Gall* and *Prof. Stephan Diehl* for being additional examiners of this thesis. Many thanks to *Prof. Raimund Seidel* and *Prof. Christoph Koch* for being scientific advisors ("wissenschaftliche Begleiter") of my research.

Very special thanks to *Silvia Breu, Valentin Dallmeier, Marc Eaddy, Sung Kim, Ben Livshits, Nachi Nagappan, Stephan Neuhaus, Rahul Premraj,* and *Andreas Zeller* for the great collaborations over the past years. Thanks a lot for your fruitful discussions and valuable comments on my research. I am looking forward to our next projects.

Many thanks to everyone who co-authored a paper with me over the past years: *Alfred V. Aho, Nicolas Bettenburg, Silvia Breu, Valentin Dallmeier, Stephan Diehl, Marc Eaddy, Vibhav Garg, Tudor Girba, Daniel Gmach, Konstantin Halachev, Ahmed Hassan, Kim Herzig, Paul Holleis, Christian Holler, Wolfgang Holz, Sascha Just, Miryung Kim, Sunghun Kim, Christian Lindig, Ben Livshits, Audris Mockus, Gail Murphy, Nachiappan Nagappan, Stephan Neuhaus, Kai Pan, Martin Pinzger, Raul Premraj, Daniel Schreck, Adrian Schröter, David Schuler, Kaitlin Sherwood, Jacek Sliwerski, Cathrin Weiss, Peter Weißgerber, Jim Whitehead,* and *Andreas Zeller.*

Thanks to all members of the software engineering group at Saarland University, including all the students that I worked with. It was a great time in Saarbrücken! Thanks to everyone who proofread one of my papers. A special thanks to *Naomi Nir-Bleimling* and *Christa Schäfer* for all their administrative help.

My doctoral studies were financially supported by a research fellowship of the DFG Research Training Group "Performance Guarantees for Computer Systems". The Graduiertenkolleg offered many opportunitites to meet other researchers and I benefited a lot by being part of it.

Many thanks to the University of Calgary for giving me a position—even before I finished my PhD. In addition, they relieved me from teaching duties, so that I could focus on the completion of my thesis. Thanks for all the confidence in my research.

Finally, and most deeply, I thank my parents, *Veronika Zimmermann* and *Prof. Walter Zimmermann*, and my sister, *Andrea Winter*, for their loving support throughout my studies.

B

Bibliography

Fernando Brito e. Abreu and Walcélio L. Melo. Evaluating the impact of object-oriented design on software quality. In *METRICS'96: Proceedings of the 3rd International Symposium on Software Metrics*, pages 90–99, 1996. See pages 84 and 103.

Rakesh Agrawal and Ramakrishnan Srikant. Fast algorithms for mining association rules in large databases. In *VLDB'94: Proceedings of the 20th International Conference on Very Large Data Bases*, pages 487–499, 1994. See pages 13 and 15.

Rajeev Alur, Pavol Černý, P. Madhusudan, and Wonhong Nam. Synthesis of interface specifications for java classes. In *POPL'05: Proceedings of the 32nd ACM SIGPLAN-SIGACT Symposium on Principles of Programming Languages*, pages 98–109, 2005. ISBN 1-58113-830-X. See page 35.

Glenn Ammons, Rastislav Bodík, and James R. Larus. Mining specifications. In *POPL'02: Proceedings of the 29th ACM SIGPLAN-SIGACT Symposium on Principles of Programming Languages*, pages 4–16, 2002. ISBN 1-58113-450-9. See page 35.

Thomas Ball, Byron Cook, Vladimir Levin, and Sriram K. Rajamani. SLAM and static driver verifier: Technology transfer of formal methods inside Microsoft. In *IFM'04:*

Proceedings of the 4th International Conference on Integrated Formal Methods, pages 1–20, 2004. See page 7.

Victor R. Basili, Lionel C. Briand, and Walcélio L. Melo. A validation of object orient design metrics as quality indicators. *IEEE Transactions on Software Engineering*, 22(10):751–761, 1996. See pages 61 and 66.

Victor R. Basili, Forrest Shull, and Filippo Lanubile. Building knowledge through families of experiments. *IEEE Transactions on Software Engineering*, 25(4):456–473, 1999. See pages 90 and 105.

Jennifer Bevan and E. James Whitehead, Jr. Identification of software instabilities. In *WCRE'03: Proceedings of the 10th Working Conference on Reverse Engineering*, pages 134–143, 2003. See pages 33 and 34.

Jennifer Bevan, Jr. E. James Whitehead, Sunghun Kim, and Michael Godfrey. Facilitating software evolution research with kenyon. In *ESEC/FSE-13: Proceedings of the 10th European Software Engineering Conference held jointly with 13th ACM SIGSOFT International Symposium on Foundations of Software Engineering*, pages 177–186, 2005. ISBN 1-59593-014-0. See page 34.

James M. Bieman, Anneliese A. Andrews, and Helen J. Yang. Understanding change-proneness in oo software through visualization. In *IWPC'03: Proceedings of the 11th IEEE International Workshop on Program Comprehension*, 2003. See pages 33 and 34.

Aaron B. Binkley and Stephen R. Schach. Validation of the coupling dependency metric as a predictor of run-time failures and maintenance measures. In *ICSE'98: Proceedings of the 20th international conference on Software engineering*, pages 452–455, 1998. See page 67.

David Binkley and Mark Harman. An empirical study of predicate dependence levels and trends. In *ICSE'03: Proceedings of the 25th International Conference on Software Engineering*, pages 330–339, 2003. ISBN 0-7695-1877-X. See page 65.

Bruno Blanchet, Patrick Cousot, Radhia Cousot, Jérome Feret, Laurent Mauborgne, Antoine Miné, David Monniaux, and Xavier Rival. A static analyzer for large safety-critical software. In *PLDI'03: Proceedings of the ACM SIGPLAN 2003 Conference on Programming Language Design and Implementation*, pages 196–207, June 2003. ISBN 1-58113-662-5. See pages 7 and 33.

Barry Boehm and Richard Turner. *Balancing Agility and Discipline: A Guide for the Perplexed*. Addison-Wesley Professional, 2003. See page 108.

Stephen P. Borgatti, Martin G. Everett, and Linton C. Freeman. Ucinet 6 for windows: Software for social network analysis. Technical report, Analytic Technologies, Harvard, 2002. See page 72.

Guillaume Brat and Arnaud Venet. Precise and scalable static program analysis of NASA flight software. In *Proceedings of the 2005 IEEE Aerospace Conference*, 2005. See pages 7 and 33.

Silvia Breu. Aspect mining using event traces. Master's thesis, University of Passau, Germany, March 2004. See page 57.

Silvia Breu. Extending dynamic aspect mining with static information. In *SCAM'05: Proceedings of the Fifth IEEE International Workshop on Source Code Analysis and Manipulation*, pages 57–65, 2005. See page 57.

Silvia Breu and Jens Krinke. Aspect mining using event traces. In *ASE'04: Proceedings of the 19th IEEE international conference on Automated software engineering*, pages 310–315, September 2004. ISBN 0-7695-2131-2. See page 57.

Lionel C. Briand, Prem Devanbu, and Walcelio Melo. An investigation into coupling measures for C++. In *ICSE'97: Proceedings of the 19th International Conference on Software Engineering*, pages 412–421, 1997. See page 66.

Coen Bron and Joep Kerbosch. Algorithm 457: finding all cliques of an undirected graph. *Communications of the ACM*, 16(9):575–577, 1973. See page 63.

Bill Burke and Adrian Brock. Aspect-oriented programming and JBoss. http://www.onjava.com/pub/a/onjava/2003/05/28/aop_jboss.html, 2003. See page 20.

Ronald Burt. *Structural Holes: The Social Structure of Competition*. Harvard University Press, 1995. See page 74.

William R. Bush, Jonathan D. Pincus, and David J. Sielaff. A static analyzer for finding dynamic programming errors. *Software – Practice and Experience (SPE)*, 30(7): 775–802, 2000. See page 32.

David Carlson. *Eclipse Distilled*. Addison-Wesley Professional, 2005. See page 23.

Junghoo Cho, Hector Garcia-Molina, and Lawrence Page. Efficient crawling through URL ordering. *Computer Networks*, 30(1-7):161–172, 1998. See page 75.

Thomas H. Cormen, Charles E. Leiserson, Ronald L. Rivest, and Clifford Stein. *Introduction to Algorithms*. The MIT Press, 2nd edition, 2001. See page 97.

Davor Cubranic, Gail C. Murphy, Janice Singer, and Kellogg S. Booth. Hipikat: A project memory for software development. *IEEE Transactions on Software Engineering*, 31(6):446–465, 2005. See pages 2 and 113.

Valentin Dallmeier, Christian Lindig, and Andreas Zeller. Lightweight defect localization for java. In *ECOOP'05: Proceedings of the 19th European Conference on Object-Oriented Programming*, pages 528–550, July 2005. See page 35.

Robert DeLine, Mary Czerwinski, and George Robertson. Easing program comprehension by sharing navigation data. In *VLHCC'05: Proceedings of the 2005 IEEE Symposium on Visual Languages and Human-Centric Computing*, pages 241–248, 2005. See page 3.

Giovanni Denaro, Sandro Morasca, and Mauro Pezzè. Deriving models of software fault-proneness. In *SEKE'02: Proceedings of the 14th International Conference on Software Engineering and Knowledge Engineering*, pages 361–368, 2002. ISBN 1-58113-556-4. See page 66.

Bill Dudney, Stephen Asbury, Joseph Krozak, and Kevin Wittkopf. *J2EE AntiPatterns*. Wiley, 2003. See page 33.

Dawson Engler, Benjamin Chelf, Andy Chou, and Seth Hallem. Checking system rules using system-specific, programmer-written compiler extensions. In *OSDI'00: Proceedings of the 4th Conference on Symposium on Operating System Design & Implementation*, pages 1–16, 2000. See pages 7, 8, 9, and 29.

Dawson Engler, David Yu Chen, Seth Hallem, Andy Chou, and Benjamin Chelf. Bugs as deviant behavior: a general approach to inferring errors in systems code. In *SOSP'01: Proceedings of the Eighteenth Acm Symposium on Operating Systems Principles*, pages 57–72, 2001. ISBN 1-58113-389-8. See pages 8, 30, and 33.

Michael D. Ernst, Jake Cockrell, William G. Griswold, and David Notkin. Dynamically discovering likely program invariants to support program evolution. *IEEE Transactions on Software Engineering*, 27(2):99–123, 2001. See page 35.

Norman E. Fenton and Niclas Ohlsson. Quantitative analysis of faults and failures in a complex software system. *IEEE Transactions on Software Engineering*, 26(8): 797–814, 2000. See pages 90 and 105.

Norman E. Fenton and Shari Lawrence Pfleeger. *Software Metrics: A Rigorous and Practical Approach.* PWS Publishing Co., 1998. See pages 78, 99, and 103.

Jeanne Ferrante, Karl J. Ottenstein, and Joe D. Warren. The program dependence graph and its use in optimization. *ACM Transactions on Programming Languages and Systems*, 9(3):319–349, 1987. See page 65.

Michael Fischer, Martin Pinzger, and Harald Gall. Populating a release history database from version control and bug tracking systems. In *ICSM'03: Proceedings of the International Conference on Software Maintenance*, pages 23–32, 2003a. ISBN 0-7695-1905-9. See page 34.

Michael Fischer, Martin Pinzger, and Harald Gall. Analyzing and relating bug report data for feature tracking. In *WCRE'03: Proceedings of the 10th Working Conference on Reverse Engineering*, pages 90–101, November 2003b. See page 34.

Beat Fluri and Harald C. Gall. Classifying change types for qualifying change couplings. In *ICPC'06: Proceedings of the 14th IEEE International Conference on Program Comprehension*, pages 35–45, 2006. ISBN 0-7695-2601-2. See page 33.

Beat Fluri, Harald C. Gall, and Martin Pinzger. Fine-grained analysis of change couplings. In *SCAM'05: Proceedings of the Fifth IEEE International Workshop on Source Code Analysis and Manipulation*, pages 66–74, 2005. ISBN 0-7695-2292-0. See page 34.

Beat Fluri, Michael Wuersch, Martin Pinzger, and Harald Gall. Change distilling:tree differencing for fine-grained source code change extraction. *IEEE Transactions on Software Engineering*, 33(11):725–743, 2007. ISSN 0098-5589. See page 33.

Harald Gall, Karin Hajek, and Mehdi Jazayeri. Detection of logical coupling based on product release history. In *ICSM'98: Proceedings of the International Conference on Software Maintenance*, pages 190–198, November 1998. See pages 18 and 34.

Harald Gall, Mehdi Jazayeri, and Jacek Krajewski. CVS release history data for detecting logical couplings. In *IWPSE'03: Proceedings of the 6th International Workshop on Principles of Software Evolution*, pages 13–23, September 2003. See pages 18, 33, and 34.

Daniel German. Mining CVS repositories, the softChange experience. In *MSR'04: Proceedings of the First International Workshop on Mining Software Repositories*, pages 17–21, 2004. See page 34.

Rishab Aiyer Ghosh. Clustering and dependencies in free/open source software development: Methodology and tools. *First Monday*, 8(4), 2003. See page 65.

Tudor Gîrba, Adrian Kuhn, Mauricio Seeberger, and Stéphane Ducasse. How developers drive software evolution. In *IWPSE'05: Proceedings of the Eighth International Workshop on Principles of Software Evolution*, pages 113–122, 2005. ISBN 0-7695-2349-8. See page 42.

Michael W. Godfrey and Lijie Zou. Using origin analysis to detect merging and splitting of source code entities. *IEEE Transactions on Software Engineering*, 31(2): 166–181, 2005. See page 46.

Todd L. Graves, Alan F. Karr, J. S. Marron, and Harvey Siy. Predicting fault incidence using software change history. *IEEE Transactions on Software Engineering*, 26(7): 653–661, 2000. See page 66.

William G. Griswold, Yoshikiyo Kato, and Jimmy J. Yuan. Aspect browser: Tool support for managing dispersed aspects. Technical Report CS1999-0640, University of California, San Diego, 1999. See page 56.

Seth Hallem, Benjamin Chelf, Yichen Xie, and Dawson Engler. A system and language for building system-specific, static analyses. In *PLDI'02: Proceedings of the ACM SIGPLAN 2002 Conference on Programming Language Design and Implementation*, pages 69–82, 2002. ISBN 1-58113-463-0. See page 33.

Robert A. Hanneman and Mark Riddle. *Introduction to social network methods*. University of California, Riverside, Riverside, CA, 2005. See pages 72 and 75.

Jan Hannemann and Gregor Kiczales. Overcoming the prevalent decomposition of legacy code. In *Workshop on Advanced Separation of Concerns in Software Engineering*, 2001. See page 56.

Ahmed E. Hassan and Richard C. Holt. The small world of software reverse engineering. In *WCRE'04: Proceedings of the 11th Working Conference on Reverse Engineering (WCRE'04)*, pages 278–283, 2004. ISBN 0-7695-2243-2. See page 65.

Reed Hastings and Bob Joyce. Purify: Fast detection of memory leaks and access errors. In *Proceedings of the Winter USENIX Conference*, pages 125–138, December 1992. See page 32.

David L. Heine and Monica S. Lam. A practical flow-sensitive and context-sensitive C and C++ memory leak detector. In *PLDI'03: Proceedings of the ACM SIGPLAN 2003 conference on Programming language design and implementation*, pages 168–181, June 2003. See pages 32 and 33.

Sallie M. Henry and Dennis G. Kafura. Software structure metrics based on information flow. *IEEE Transactions on Software Engineering*, 7(5):510–518, 1981. See page 65.

Shih-Kun Huang and Kang-Min Liu. Mining version histories to verify the learning process of legitimate peripheral participants. In *MSR'05: Proceedings of the 2005 International Workshop on Mining Software Repositories*, 2005. See page 65.

Yao-Wen Huang, Fang Yu, Christian Hang, Chung-Hung Tsai, Der-Tsai Lee, and Sy-Yen Kuo. Securing web application code by static analysis and runtime protection. In *WWW'04: Proceedings of the 13th Conference on World Wide Web*, pages 40–52, May 2004. See page 7.

E.J. Jackson. *A Users Guide to Principal Components*. John Wiley & Sons Inc., Hoboken, NJ, 2003. See pages 82 and 102.

Huzefa H. Kagdi, Michael L. Collard, and Jonathan I. Maletic. A survey and taxonomy of approaches for mining software repositories in the context of software evolution. *Journal of Software Maintenance*, 19(2):77–131, 2007. See page 1.

Taghi M. Khoshgoftaar, Edward B. Allen, Nishith Goel, Amit Nandi, and John Mc-Mullan. Detection of software modules with high debug code churn in a very large legacy system. In *ISSRE'96: Proceedings of the Seventh International Symposium on Software Reliability Engineering*, pages 364–371, 1996. See page 66.

Gregor Kiczales, John Lamping, Anurag Mendhekar, Chris Maeda, Cristina Videira Lopes, Jean-Marc Loingtier, and John Irwin. Aspect-oriented programming. In *ECOOP'97: Proceedings of the 11th European Conference on Object-Oriented Programming*, pages 220–242, 1997. See page 37.

Miryung Kim and David Notkin. Program element matching for multi-version program analyses. In *MSR'06: Proceedings of the 2006 international workshop on Mining software repositories*, pages 58–64, 2006. ISBN 1-59593-397-2. See page 33.

Sunghun Kim, E. James Whitehead, and Jennifer Bevan. Analysis of signature change patterns. In *MSR'05: Proceedings of the 2005 International Workshop on Mining Software Repositories*, 2005. See page 33.

Sunghun Kim, Kai Pan, and E. James Whitehead, Jr. Memories of bug fixes. In *SIGSOFT'06/FSE-14: Proceedings of the 14th ACM SIGSOFT International Symposium on Foundations of Software Engineering*, pages 35–45, 2006. See pages 112 and 114.

Andrew J. Ko and Brad A. Myers. A framework and methodology for studying the causes of software errors in programming systems. *Journal of Visual Languages and Computing*, 16(1-2):41–84, 2005. See page 108.

Bogdan Korel. The program dependence graph in static program testing. *Information Processing Letters*, 24(2):103–108, 1987. See page 65.

Jens Krinke and Silvia Breu. Control-flow-graph-based aspect mining. In *WARE'04: Workshop on Aspect Reverse Engineering*, November 2004. See page 56.

Sanjeev Kumar and Kai Li. Using model checking to debug device firmware. In *OSDI'02: Proceedings of the 5th symposium on Operating systems design and implementation*, pages 61–74, 2002. See page 33.

Patrick Lam and Martin Rinard. A type system and analysis for the automatic extraction and enforcement of design information. In *ECOOP'03: Proceedings of the 17th European Conference on Object-Oriented Programming*, pages 275–302, July 2003. See page 35.

Zhenmin Li, Lin Tan, Xuanhui Wang, Shan Lu, Yuanyuan Zhou, and Chengxiang Zhai. Have things changed now? An empirical study of bug characteristics in modern open source software. In *ASID'06: Proceedings of the 1st workshop on Architectural and system support for improving software dependability*, pages 25–33, 2006. ISBN 1-59593-576-2. See page 62.

Benjamin Livshits and Thomas Zimmermann. DynaMine: finding common error patterns by mining software revision histories. In *ESEC/FSE-13: Proceedings of the 10th European Software Engineering conference held jointly with 13th ACM SIGSOFT International Symposium on Foundations of Software Engineering*, pages 296–305, 2005. ISBN 1-59593-014-0. See pages 40 and 46.

Luis Lopez-Fernandez, Gregorio Robles, and Jesus M. Gonzalez-Barahona. Applying social network analysis to the information in CVS repositories. In *MSR'04: Proceedings of the First International Workshop on Mining Software Repositories*, pages 101–105, 2004. See page 65.

Neil Loughran and Awais Rashid. Mining aspects. In *Workshop on Early Aspects: Aspect-Oriented Requirements Engineering and Architecture Design*, 2002. See page 57.

Greg Madey, Vincent Freeh, and Renee Tynan. The open source software development phenomenon: An analysis based on social network theory. *AMCIS'02: Americas Conference on Information Systems*, pages 1806–1813, 2002. See page 65.

Heikki Mannila, Hannu Toivonen, and A. Inkeri Verkamo. Efficient algorithms for discovering association rules. In *KDD' 94: Proceedings of the AAAI Workshop on Knowledge Discovery in Databases*, pages 181–192, July 1994. See pages 13 and 15.

Marius Marin, Arie van Deursen, and Leon Moonen. Identifying aspects using fan-in analysis. In *WCRE'04: Proceedings of the 11th Working Conference on Reverse Engineering*, pages 132–141, 2004. ISBN 0-7695-2243-2. See page 57.

Marius Marin, Leon Moonen, and Arie van Deursen. A classification of crosscutting concerns. In *ICSM'05: Proceedings of the 21st IEEE International Conference on Software Maintenance*, pages 673–676, 2005. ISBN 0-7695-2368-4. See page 55.

Marius Marin, Arie van Deursen, and Leon Moonen. Identifying crosscutting concerns using fan-in analysis. *ACM Transactions on Software Engineering and Methodology*, 17(1), 2007. See page 57.

David W. McDonald and Mark S. Ackerman. Expertise recommender: a flexible recommendation system and architecture. In *CSCW'00: Proceedings of the 2000 ACM Conference on Computer Supported Cooperative Work*, pages 231–240, 2000. See page 114.

Amir Michail. Data mining library reuse patterns using generalized association rules. In *ICSE'00: Proceedings of the 22nd international conference on Software engineering*, pages 167–176, June 2000. ISBN 1-58113-206-9. See pages 16 and 34.

Amir Michail. Data mining library reuse patterns in user-selected applications. In *ASE'99: Proceedings of the 14th IEEE international conference on Automated software engineering*, pages 24–33, October 1999. See pages 16 and 34.

R. Milo, S. Shen-Orr, S. Itzkovitz, N. Kashtan, D. Chklovskii, and U. Alon. Network motifs: Simple building blocks of complex networks. *Science*, 298(5594):824–827, 2002. See page 63.

Audris Mockus and James D. Herbsleb. Expertise browser: a quantitative approach to identifying expertise. In *ICSE'02: Proceedings of the 24th International Conference on Software Engineering*, pages 503–512, 2002. See page 114.

Audris Mockus and David M. Weiss. Predicting risk of software changes. *Bell Labs Technical Journal*, 5(2):169–180, 2000. See page 33.

Audris Mockus, Ping Zhang, and Paul Li. Predictors of customer perceived software quality. In *ICSE'05: Proceedings of the 27th International Conference on Software Engineering*, pages 225–233, 2005. See page 66.

John C. Munson and Taghi M. Khoshgoftaar. The detection of fault-prone programs. *IEEE Transactions on Software Engineering*, 18(5):423–433, 1992. See pages 83 and 102.

Karl-Heinrich Möller and Daniel J. Paulish. An empirical investigation of software fault distribution. In *METRICS'93: Proceedings of the First International Software Metrics Symposium*, pages 82–90, 1993. See pages 90 and 105.

Nachiappan Nagappan and Thomas Ball. Use of relative code churn measures to predict system defect density. In *ICSE'05: Proceedings of the 27th International Conference on Software Engineering*, pages 284–292, 2005. See page 107.

Nachiappan Nagappan and Thomas Ball. Using software dependencies and churn metrics to predict field failures: An empirical case study. In *ESEM'07: Proceedings of the First International Symposium on Empirical Software Engineering and Measurement*, pages 364–373, 2007. ISBN 0-7695-2886-4. See page 66.

Nachiappan Nagappan, Thomas Ball, and Andreas Zeller. Mining metrics to predict component failures. In *ICSE'06: Proceeding of the 28th international conference on Software engineering*, pages 452–461, 2006a. See page 112.

Nachiappan Nagappan, Thomas Ball, and Andreas Zeller. Mining metrics to predict component failures. In *ICSE'06: Proceedings of the 28th International Conference on Software Engineering*, pages 452–461, 2006b. See pages 61, 67, 90, 105, and 107.

N.J.D. Nagelkerke. A note on a general definition of the coefficient of determination. *Biometrika*, 78:691–692, 1991. See page 83.

Iulian Neamtiu, Jeffrey S. Foster, and Michael Hicks. Understanding source code evolution using abstract syntax tree matching. In *MSR'05: Proceedings of the 2005 international workshop on Mining software repositories*, pages 1–5, 2005. ISBN 1-59593-123-6. See page 33.

Nicholas Nethercote and Julian Seward. Valgrind: A program supervision framework. *Electronic Notes in Theoretical Computer Science*, 89, 2003. See page 32.

Masao Ohira, Naoki Ohsugi, Tetsuya Ohoka, and Ken ichi Matsumoto. Accelerating cross-project knowledge collaboration using collaborative filtering and social networks. In *MSR'05: Proceedings of the 2005 International Workshop on Mining Software Repositories*, 2005. See page 65.

Niclas Ohlsson and Hans Alberg. Predicting fault-prone software modules in telephone switches. *IEEE Transactions on Software Engineering*, 22(12):886–894, 1996. See page 67.

Ales Orso, Saurabh Sinha, and Mary Jean Harrold. Classifying data dependences in the presence of pointers for program comprehension, testing, and debugging. *ACM Transactions on Software Engineering and Methodology*, 13(2):199–239, 2004. See page 65.

Thomas J Ostrand, Elaine J. Weyuker, and Robert M. Bell. Predicting the location and number of faults in large software systems. *IEEE Transactions on Software Engineering*, 31(4):340–355, 2005. See pages 66, 90, and 105.

Slava Pestov. jEdit user guide. http://www.jedit.org/, 2007. See page 23.

Martin Pinzger, Michael Fischer, and Harald C. Gall. Towards an integrated view on architecture and its evolution. *Electronic Notes in Theoretical Computer Science*, 127(3):183–196, April 2005. See page 114.

Andy Pogdurski and Lori A. Clarke. A formal model of program dependences and its implications for software testing, debugging, and maintenance. *IEEE Transactions on Software Engineering*, 16(9):965–979, 1990. See page 65.

Ranjith Purushothaman and Dewayne E. Perry. Toward understanding the rhetoric of small source code changes. *IEEE Transactions on Software Engineering*, 31(6): 511–526, 2005. See pages 10 and 19.

Brian Randell. System structure for software fault tolerance. *IEEE Transactions on Software Engineering*, 1(2):221–232, 1975. See page 87.

Darrell Reimer, Edith Schonberg, Kavitha Srinivas, Harini Srinivasan, Bowen Alpern, Robert D. Johnson, Aaron Kershenbaum, and Larry Koved. SABER: Smart analysis based error reduction. In *ISSTA'04: Proceedings of the 2004 ACM SIGSOFT International Symposium on Software Testing and Analysis*, pages 243–251, July 2004. See pages 8 and 33.

Filip Van Rysselberghe and Serge Demeyer. Mining version control systems for FACs (frequently applied changes). In *MSR'04: Proceedings of the First International Workshop on Mining Software Repositories*, pages 48–52, May 2004. See page 16.

Tobias Sager, Abraham Bernstein, Martin Pinzger, and Christoph Kiefer. Detecting similar java classes using tree algorithms. In *MSR'06: Proceedings of the 2006 international workshop on Mining software repositories*, pages 65–71, 2006. ISBN 1-59593-397-2. See page 33.

Stefan Savage, Michael Burrows, Greg Nelson, Patrick Sobalvarro, and Thomas Anderson. Eraser: a dynamic data race detector for multithreaded programs. *ACM Transactions on Computer Systems (TOCS)*, 15(4):391–411, 1997. ISSN 0734-2071. See page 32.

Stephen R. Schach. *Object-Oriented and Classical Software Engineering*. McGraw-Hill Science/Engineering/Math, 6th edition, 2004. See pages 28 and 35.

Daniel Schreck, Valentin Dallmeier, and Thomas Zimmermann. How documentation evolves over time. In *IWPSE'07: Proceedings of the 9th International Workshop on Principles of Software Evolution*, pages 4–10, September 2007. See page 114.

Adrian Schröter, Thomas Zimmermann, and Andreas Zeller. Predicting component failures at design time. In *ISESE'06: Proceedings of the 2006 ACM/IEEE International Symposium on International Symposium on Empirical Software Engineering*, pages 18–27, 2006. ISBN 1-59593-218-6. See pages 66 and 79.

Adrian Schröter, Thomas Zimmermann, and Andreas Zeller. Predicting component failures at design time. In *ISESE'06: Proceedings of the 5th ACM-IEEE International Symposium on Empirical Software Engineering*, pages 18–27, September 2006. See page 113.

Umesh Shankar, Kunal Talwar, Jeffrey S. Foster, and David Wagner. Detecting format string vulnerabilities with type qualifiers. In *Proceedings of the 2001 Usenix Security Conference*, pages 201–220, 2001. See pages 8 and 33.

David Shepherd and Lori Pollock. Ophir: A framework for automatic mining and refactoring of aspects. Technical Report 2004-03, University of Delaware, 2003. See page 56.

Janice Singer, Robert Elves, and Margaret-Anne Storey. NavTracks: Supporting navigation in software maintenance. In *ICSM'05: Proceedings of the 21st IEEE International Conference on Software Maintenance*, pages 325–334, 2005. See page 3.

Saurabh Sinha, Mary Jean Harrold, and Gregg Rothermel. Interprocedural control dependence. *ACM Transactions on Software Engineering and Methodology*, 10(2): 209–254, 2001. See page 65.

Amitabh Srivastava, Jay Thiagarajan, and Craig Schertz. Efficient integration testing using dependency analysis. Technical Report MSR-TR-2005-94, Microsoft Research, 2005. See pages 70 and 71.

Ramanath Subramanyam and Mayuram S. Krishnan. Empirical analysis of ck metrics for object-oriented design complexity: Implications for software defects. *IEEE Transactions on Software Engineering*, 29(4):297–310, 2003. See pages 61 and 66.

Peri Tarr, Harold Ossher, William Harrison, and Stanley M. Sutton, Jr. N degrees of separation: Multi-dimensional separation of concerns. In *ICSE'99: Proceedings of the 21st international conference on Software engineering*, pages 107–119, 1999. ISBN 1-58113-074-0. See page 37.

Gregory Tassey. The economic impacts of inadequate infrastructure for software testing. Technical report, National Institute of Standards and Technology, 2002. See page 61.

Bruce Tate, Mike Clark, Bob Lee, and Patrick Linskey. *Bitter EJB*. Manning Publications, 2003. See page 33.

Paolo Tonella and Mariano Ceccato. Aspect mining through the formal concept analysis of execution traces. In *WCRE'04: Proceedings of the 11th Working Conference on Reverse Engineering*, pages 112–121, 2004. ISBN 0-7695-2243-2. See page 57.

Tom Tourwé and Kim Mens. Mining aspectual views using formal concept analysis. In *SCAM'04: Proceedings of the Source Code Analysis and Manipulation, Fourth IEEE International Workshop on*, pages 97–106, 2004. See page 56.

Gina Venolia. Textual alusions to artifacts in software-related repositories. In *MSR'06: Proceedings of the 2006 International Workshop on Mining Software Repositories*, pages 151–154, May 2006a. See page 2.

Gina Venolia. Bridges between silos: A microsoft research project. Technical report, Microsoft Research, January 2006b. White paper. See page 2.

David Wagner, Jeffrey S. Foster, Eric A. Brewer, and Alexander Aiken. A first step towards automated detection of buffer overrun vulnerabilities. In *NDSS'00: Proceedings of the Network and Distributed System Security Symposium*, pages 3–17, February 2000. See pages 7 and 33.

Stanley Wasserman and Katherine Faust. *Social Network Analysis: Methods and Applications*. Cambridge University Press, Cambridge, 1984. See pages 72 and 75.

Westley Weimer and George Necula. Mining temporal specifications for error detection. In *TACAS'05: Proceedings of the 11th International Conference on Tools and Algorithms for the Construction and Analysis of Systems*, pages 461–476, April 2005. See page 35.

Peter Weißgerber and Stephan Diehl. Identifying refactorings from source-code changes. In *ASE'06: Proceedings of the 21st IEEE International Conference on Automated Software Engineering*, pages 231–240, 2006. See page 114.

Douglas B. West. *Introduction to Graph Theory*. Prentice Hall, 2nd edition, 2001. See page 97.

John Whaley, Michael C. Martin, and Monica S. Lam. Automatic extraction of object-oriented component interfaces. In *ISSTA'02: Proceedings of the 2002 ACM SIG-SOFT international symposium on Software testing and analysis*, pages 218–228, July 2002. See page 35.

Chadd C. Williams and Jeffrey K. Hollingsworth. Recovering system specific rules from software repositories. In *MSR'05: Proceedings of the 2005 International Workshop on Mining Software Repositories*, pages 7–11, May 2005a. See pages 19, 34, and 57.

Chadd C. Williams and Jeffrey K. Hollingsworth. Automatic mining of source code repositories to improve bug finding techniques. *IEEE Transactions on Software Engineering*, 31(6):466–480, June 2005b. See pages 19, 34, and 46.

Tao Xie and Jian Pei. MAPO: Mining API usages from open source repositories. In *MSR'06: Proceedings of the 2006 International Workshop on Mining Software Repositories*, pages 54–57, May 2006. See page 46.

Yunwen Ye and Gerhard Fischer. Supporting reuse by delivering task-relevant and personalized information. In *ICSE'02: Proceedings of the 24th International Conference on Software Engineering*, pages 513–523, 2002. See page 113.

Annie T.T. Ying, Gail C. Murphy, Raymond Ng, and Mark C. Chu-Carroll. Predicting source code changes by mining change history. *IEEE Transactions on Software Engineering*, 30(9):574–586, September 2004. See page 34.

Thomas Zimmermann. Fine-grained processing of CVS archives with APFEL. In *eclipse'06: Proceedings of the 2006 OOPSLA workshop on eclipse technology eXchange*, pages 16–20, 2006. ISBN 1-59593-621-1. See page 34.

Thomas Zimmermann and Peter Weißgerber. Preprocessing CVS data for fine-grained analysis. In *MSR'04: Proceedings of the First International Workshop on Mining Software Repositories*, pages 2–6, May 2004. See pages 19, 34, and 45.

Thomas Zimmermann, Stephan Diehl, and Andreas Zeller. How history justifies system architecture (or not). In *IWPSE'03: Proceedings of the 6th International Workshop on Principles of Software Evolution*, pages 73–83, Helsinki, Finland, September 2003. See pages 18, 33, and 34.

Thomas Zimmermann, Peter Weißgerber, Stephan Diehl, and Andreas Zeller. Mining version histories to guide software changes. *IEEE Transactions on Software Engineering*, 31(6):429–445, June 2005. See pages 3 and 34.

About this Book

Software development results in a huge amount of data: changes to source code are recorded in version archives, bugs are reported to issue tracking systems, and communications are archived in e-mails and newsgroups. This book presents techniques for mining version archives and bug databases to better understand and support software development.

First, we present techniques which mine version archives for fine-grained changes. We introduce the concept of co-addition of method calls, which we use to identify patterns that describe how methods should be called. We use dynamic analysis to validate these patterns and identify violations. The co-addition of method calls can also detect cross-cutting changes, which are an indicator for concerns that could have been realized as aspects in aspect-oriented programming.

Second, we present techniques to build models that can successfully predict the most defect-prone parts in large-scale industrial software, in our study Windows Server 2003. This helps managers to allocate resources for quality assurance to those parts of a system that are expected to have most defects. The proposed measures on dependency graphs outperformed traditional complexity metrics. In addition, we found empirical evidence for a domino effect: depending on defect-prone binaries increases the chances of having defects.

About the Author

Thomas Zimmermann is a researcher at Microsoft Research, USA, and an adjunct assistant professor at the University of Calgary, Canada. His work involves the evolution of large, complex software systems, conducting empirical studies and building tools that use data mining to support developers and managers. He received his PhD in computer science from Saarland University, Germany. Contact him at tz@acm.org.

About this Book in a Wordle

www.ingramcontent.com/pod-product-compliance
Lightning Source LLC
LaVergne TN
LVHW080117070326
832902LV00015B/2638